Experiences
of Divine Love
IN THE COMPANY OF
A MODERN PROPHET

D1160821

Experiences *of* Divine Love

IN THE COMPANY OF A MODERN PROPHET

Jon Uan

ECKANKAR
Minneapolis
www.Eckankar.org

Experiences of Divine Love
in the Company of a Modern Prophet

Copyright © 2012 Jon Uan

All rights reserved. No part of this book may be reproduced, stored in a retrieval system, or transmitted in any form by any means, whether electronic, mechanical, photocopying, recording, or otherwise, without prior written permission of Eckankar.

The terms ECKANKAR, ECK, EK, MAHANTA, SOUL TRAVEL, and VAIRAGI, among others, are trademarks of ECKANKAR, PO Box 2000, Chanhassen, MN 55317-2000 USA.   081239

Printed in USA

Edited by Patrick Carroll, Joan Klemp, and Anthony Moore
Cover illustration by Claude Gruffy
Cover design by Stan Burgess and Doug Munson

Library of Congress Cataloging-in-Publication Data

Uan, Jon.
    Experiences of divine love in the company of a modern prophet /
Jon Uan.
       p. cm.
    Summary: "Nigerian author Jon Uan's account of getting
help in his daily life through dreams, miracles, and spiritual
experiences in Eckankar with Sri Harold Klemp, the Mahanta,
the Living ECK Master"—Provided by publisher.
    Includes bibliographical references (p.   ).
    ISBN 978-1-57043-312-2 (pbk. : alk. paper)
    1. Uan, Jon. 2. Eckankar (Organization)—Biography. 3.
Eckankar (Organization)—Doctrines. 4. Klemp, Harold.   I. Title.
BP605.E3U26 2012
299'.93—dc23
                                        2012006955

♾ This paper meets the requirements of ANSI/NISO Z39.48-1992
(Permanence of Paper).

Contents

Acknowledgments

Thanks to the "double basketball team"—Aza, Koko, Ayugus, Inyon, Adonko, Dr. Chef, Akume Kor, Agabus, Ubogu, and Igiladu—for providing the challenges of fatherhood!

And to "First Lady," who often waited alone in bed while this book cooked!

And to "Philosopher" Joe, for doing the buying while I did the reading!

Let's not forget Mchivga, for giving inspiration unconsciously!

To the Mahanta, the Living ECK Master and the order of ECK Masters—there would have been no such book without you!

Introduction

Experiences of Divine Love in the Company of a Modern Prophet is based on my personal experiences as a follower of the teachings of Eckankar, Religion of the Light and Sound of God.

I started recording these experiences when I heeded an inner nudge and began keeping a dream journal on May 31, 1991. Little did I realize at the time that I was beginning a very serious study about the spiritual nature of all life and of myself as Soul, a divine spark of God.

The Mahanta, the Living ECK Master Sri Harold Klemp is a modern prophet and the spiritual leader of Eckankar. As my spiritual guide, he is thus the moving spirit behind the events in this book.

During my studies, I've had countless insights, but the following three points are, to me, key to the teachings of Eckankar.

1. The Chief Agent of God

   The chief agent of God is known in Eckankar as the Mahanta. He exists in a physical form, a human body, as the Living ECK Master. Yet as the Mahanta, the Inner Master, he is an expression of the Spirit of God that is always with us.

   In *The Shariyat-Ki-Sugmad*, the holy book of Eckankar, it says this of the Mahanta: "There is never a time when the world is without a Mahanta, the Living ECK Master, for God manifests Itself again and again in the embodiment of the chosen one. It is constant and always in the worlds."[1]

2. Travels from Earth into the Heavens

    In Eckankar, the ECK Masters help a student reach dimensions, or planes, beyond the physical realm via Soul Travel. By practicing certain spiritual exercises, one learns to suspend physical activity temporarily, as in sleep, and connect with the Light and Sound (Divine Spirit) of God. As Soul, one then shifts awareness to one of the inner bodies, which he already has on each plane of existence.

    Our nightly dreams are often partial memories of the inner travels we do naturally when asleep. Via Soul Travel, we can journey to the inner planes, from earth to the heavens, in full consciousness.

3. The Supremacy of Love and Service

    Life is all about realizing spiritual freedom, becoming a Co-worker with God, learning to give and receive divine love. During our inner travels in Eckankar, the Master removes unnecessary problems (karma) and hones our talents. We gain progressive freedom to serve God and our fellow beings better!

What follows is the story of key parts of my spiritual journey thus far. I've organized my experiences by themes, rather than chronologically; I hope this will help the reader better understand the meaning behind the events.

Part One

---✨---

Encounter with the Chief Agent of God

1
Wake-Up Calls

Sometimes God's love needs to shake the sleeping Soul and awaken It because this is the lifetime that Soul has chosen to awaken to truth. And Soul is often in a very deep sleep. It needs one spiritual jolt after another to finally become aware that there is more to life than what meets the eye.

—Harold Klemp,
How to Survive Spiritually in Our Times,
Mahanta Transcripts, Book 16[1]

My first in a series of wake-up calls came when I was still a preschool-age boy in a rural community in central Nigeria. These wake-up calls continued to young adulthood, but they took on meaning only about fifteen years before the time of this writing.

Land of Dreams

As a child, I had to go to bed early. My secret fears about going to bed early, which I could not discuss with the adults, concerned strange journeys I found myself

3

making in the land of dreams—apparently before I even fell asleep!

I would lie down in the bamboo bed, and within minutes it would feel as if I had fallen through the bed into what at first seemed like a dark, bottomless void with firefly specks in it. Finally I would emerge in a forest where it was high noon with no wind stirring; yet it was never hot.

My companion during the journey and at arrival was a sound—the trill of a tree cricket.

After landing in this forest, I would walk to the edge of a clearing about four football fields wide and stretching from horizon to horizon. The whole clearing, as far as the eye could see, was covered with graves upon graves—thousands, perhaps millions of them standing like silent witnesses to the supremacy of the Angel of Death.

Where was I? How did I get here? What brought me here? And why? I would ask myself.

Trips to Heaven

Only in middle age did I get the answers I sought. By then, I had benefited from a method of spiritual travel known only in the teachings of Eckankar. It is called Soul Travel.

The trill of the cricket was one of the innumerable sounds of the Holy Spirit, the Voice of God that facilitates such Soul journeys.

I had been brought into that forest as a reminder of the spiritual mission I had in this life: to finally be free of reincarnation in the land of death and reincarnation. The graves gave me an idea of how long I had been here. Each grave represented a single lifetime. As Soul, I was not exactly a spring chicken!

The Mahanta, chief agent of God and spiritual leader

of Eckankar, was the secret facilitator of these trips. His sole job is to lead ready Souls out of the land of life and death into a place where death and dissolution does not exist. Apparently, I was ready. But, at the time, how could I know what I didn't know? Therefore other reminders followed.

Egg in Your Face

In primary school, I stumbled on the fact that I could know what my five physical senses didn't. I was at first confused, then endangered, then elated!

In our primary-boarding-school dormitory, we lived five to a thatched round hut. The oldest, most senior boy, called householder, walked into our dorm one day with the air of a UN social worker coming into a starving refugee camp.

"Five eggs here—an egg for each member of the house," he announced, holding out a pouch. Animal protein was rare in this boarding facility that was run on a shoestring budget.

The hurrah had hardly died down when I heard myself say, to my own surprise, "Only one is good!"

Four frosty pairs of eyes turned on me.

I had not the slightest idea why I had the urge to say what I said. My face had been buried inside the straw pillow. I had not even seen the eggs he brought in, much less touched them. Why did I then prophesy such doom for an act that was so well intended?

"Get up and boil the eggs," the householder hissed. "And for every error in your prophecy, Asue here will give you a knock with his knuckles on your coconut head!"

There were just two things Asue was good at in school. One was soccer. The other was knocking smart alecks on the head. Many, including me, thought he enjoyed the latter more. It compensated for his lack of intellect.

It was useless reporting this bullying to the authorities. Like a prison, the place had its house rules beyond the reach of the law. The mafia in this boarding facility were very patient. If you reported a beating, there could come a time when a faceless group would maul you in the dark of night, then wait to see who you would accuse before the authorities next day. It was often kinder to oneself to keep mum and be careful. And I had just forgotten to be careful!

Very worried, I carried the five eggs outside and put some kindling together to boil them. While I waited for the fire to catch, I idly placed the five eggs in a basin of water. One sank and four floated.

There could possibly be something to my prophecy, I mused.

If I had known what was to happen next, I would have marked that single egg that sank before boiling them, because after boiling, all five eggs sank in the water! Only years later, in secondary-school physics, did I come to understand this phenomenon.

Good eggs contain little gas, so they sink. Bad eggs, however, contain gases like hydrogen sulphide, so they float in water. The process of boiling drives out the gases through the porous shell of the egg. And hence, the good and bad eggs became indistinguishable in my "water test."

Other Senses

I had thought the householder would simply break all five eggs and pass judgment—in my favor, hopefully.

However, a more rigorous lesson awaited me—and

them also, as it turned out. The householder would have me identify the state of each egg as he picked them at random from a basin! When I returned with the eggs, a judge's bench had been set up. I was ordered to place the five eggs in a basin as a court exhibit. The court officials were: householder, judge; Asue, executioner; and two older boys, police on each flank so I wouldn't bolt during my sentencing.

Till I discovered Eckankar almost thirty years later, I had no idea how I correctly evaluated each egg, with my eyes closed, as they were picked from the basin! I pronounced only the fourth egg good—and it turned out to be so.

Neither my adversaries nor I could believe it, and we wanted to put it down to happenstance. But could happenstance have scored five out of five?

I slipped out of the hut, pretending I wanted to get rid of the foul contents of the dustbin. I really wanted to find a place to celebrate my great escape and review my lessons.

One lesson was that I had more than the five senses! The second was to cool it on prophecy.

Divine Justice

My father once did a juggling act with divine justice in my presence, and it got me thinking—for almost thirty years.

There was no official birth registry in our part of central Nigeria when I was born. But to move from primary to secondary school, I had to present a birth certificate. The only alternative was for my father to go to the district officer, be sworn in, and get a declaration-of-age document.

Swem or the Bible?

"Will you swear on the Swem or the Bible?" the district officer asked my father.

"The Bible," my father answered quickly, much to my surprise.

I turned sharply and looked at him. He avoided my eyes and looked straight at the district officer. I knew I had to go along with him if I intended to escape ear pulling after this performance before the district officer.

My father was a follower of traditional religion. He should have sworn on the Swem, the swearing altar of our ancestors, not the Bible. Why did he choose the Bible? I asked him later.

He smiled, a mischievous twinkle in his eyes.

"I did not personally witness your birth, did I? Why take a chance with something as potent as Swem?"

"But you took the same chance on the Bible," I observed.

"Have you not seen and heard Christians swear on the Bible in court and end up telling a pack of lies thereafter? What happens to them?" he asked. "On the other hand, I have seen people who think they can lie to Swem," he chuckled mirthlessly, shaking his head. "The heap of earth where they are buried is witness to the power of Swem!"

Universal Law of Truth

My aim for telling this story here is not to endorse my father's opinion about the two religions. But I was an inexperienced preteen youth, and it got me thinking.

How does God administer the law? Is it hell on the last day, as Christians say; or daily, as the adherents of Swem believe? More important, Does divine justice depend on which God one swears upon as witness?

My father's apparent blasphemy had triggered in me an instinctive search for the universal Law of Karma—a law that has always been in operation since the beginning of time.

It was therefore easy for me to recognize and accept it later, when I encountered it in Eckankar.

Secret Communication

Whether or not he can see the form of the Master, he must try to hold a conversation through mental whisperings. He should listen for the answers which come via the intuitive or the mental arena. He should never be in doubt that the Master has spoken to him from the inner world.

The Shariyat-Ki-Sugmad, Books One & Two[2]

When we left secondary school, I went into a preparatory school for university. My best friend went into the labor market in Kaduna, a six- or seven-hour drive from our home. He promised to write, but he never did. I knew why. He hates writing.

I decided to pay him a visit—without an address and with money for just a one-way ticket!

In Kaduna, I would find someone I knew who also knew him. That person would lead me to him.

I thought I had a beautiful, workable plan—till I got to Kaduna.

More than a thousand people milled around the platform; some were arriving and others departing. The rest had come to see relatives arrive or depart among a potpourri of hawkers and motor touts.

I walked back and forth on the platform in this frenzied atmosphere, playing my last and only card—looking for someone I knew who also knew Joe.

No one turned up.

For the first time, I felt the absence of return fare in my pocket and realized the utter foolishness and madness of my travel plans.

Inner Guide Speaks Out

I was leaning against a large tree, watching the scene like an alien that had landed on planet Earth, when an impulse inside me spoke clearly:

Get on that bus!

I looked up, and the nudge became specific: *Yeah, that one over there!* It was one out of twenty or so.

I walked over quietly, boarded, and found a seat.

I felt intuitively that speaking to anyone was superfluous and perhaps even counterproductive.

The bus soon filled up, and we started on the journey—perhaps to the moon, as far as I knew.

There are bus stops on Nigerian roads, of course. But Nigerian bus drivers often create instant bus stops wherever a passenger wishes to embark or disembark. Horns may honk, and inconvenienced co-users of the road might shout obscenities, but the Nigerian bus driver takes this as an acceptable hazard in his line of business.

Every time a passenger wanted to disembark, I observed that he would rap his knuckles on the hard roof of the bus. The driver would then respond by immediately pulling to a stop.

As I watched all this in silence, that inner guide once more spoke out: *Get out now!* My knuckles went to the roof.

I disembarked a short distance from a T-junction and walked toward it. When I got there, the inner nudge said: *Turn left at this junction!* I obeyed, by this time thoroughly amused.

Two or three blocks down this road, I saw what I had looked for in vain at the train station—a known face. Someone I knew was walking toward me.

I got through the pleasantries quickly, then made my confession.

Morning of Surprises

"I am visiting Kaduna for the first time, to see Joe." Feeling foolish, I asked, "Do you have any idea where he lives?"

It must have been a morning of surprises for both of us. His eyebrows shot up in amazement. Mine were to follow shortly. Turning like a soldier doing an about-turn on the parade ground, he pointed to a door a few steps from where we stood.

"That," he said, "is the door to Joe's apartment!"

Joe was having a late Saturday-morning sleep-in. He opened the door, rubbing sleep out of his eyes. Seeing me probably made him think he was still in the dream worlds. "How did you find this place?" he asked.

"It's a long story," I said. *And an unbelievable one*, I thought.

For years afterward, I would try again and again to calculate the odds involved in this phenomenon—the odds of taking the right bus, getting off at the right time, turning the right way at the intersection, and finding this fellow I knew on that spot. Nothing explained it— till I came upon Eckankar twenty years later.

Dreams of Coming Changes

By 1984, I began to have dreams that indicated my life was about to change. But I didn't take notice. It was a time when "one for the road" (or maybe two) was more important than dreams.

After my university education, I went into the Youth Service and later worked for a year in a private architectural consultancy firm in Kano.

When I started my consultancy in architecture, I had no name, no powerful backers, no money. Yet my dreams were to succeed and own a ten-seater private Learjet! With that jet, I would shuttle around the financial capitals of the world, looking after my international business enterprise.

A tall dream for a former poor village boy whose parents could barely pay his school fees and whose only clothes, at times, were the school uniform. Yet I believed in that dream implicitly.

By the end of 1984, it was looking less and less like a laughable dream.

After working on a number of private residences and estates, I landed a commission to do a bank, followed by a hotel to be run by the Sheraton chain. During Nigeria's economically heady days, the naira was 150 percent stronger than the US dollar. Earnings in naira had international clout. My Learjet, I was sure, was just around the corner at the Makurdi Airport! But this was the time that the dreams about the coming change began.

Warnings

I am climbing stairs from the ground floor to the floor above. When I arrive, I only find a blank wall. Disappointed, I turn around to descend the stairs, but I find a rude surprise awaiting me.

I was looking for a door to the stairwell, but someone must have come on the sly and cut the stairs away, leaving me on a tiny ledge. I feel like I am hanging on a cliff. With no door to go in and no means to descend, I wake up sweating and trembling.

This dream went on for a whole year, then gave way

to another that persisted for just as long.

I watch an airplane flying into a perfect sunset. The silver arrow flies straight and true till a telltale sign of trouble shows up—smoke from the tail. Like an inebriated fly, the craft goes into a crazy dance in the sky. The plane crashes to the jungle below. The boom and flames shooting skyward awaken me, heart pounding and body trembling.

The stairs dream meant that I would climb to the next level on the spiritual spiral of life. Opportunities here would be very unfamiliar, yet retreat was impossible. Soul had burnt Its bridges!

The second dream meant that my old life would end in devastation. The Learjet dream would crash.

Waking Dreams

When I failed to heed these warnings, waking dreams took over. Fire began to follow me wherever I traveled.

Within a period of three months or so in 1985, three places I happened to be in—on three different continents—caught fire!

First Fire

The first fire happened in Bayswater, London.

I was on a business trip with my partner and the company lawyer. To reduce hotel bills, we rented a sixth-floor serviced apartment in Bayswater for a week.

We were having a party in the evening, when the doorbell rang. When we answered it, no one was there. Perhaps an electrical malfunction, we thought—not worth spilling a drink over. So we continued with the party.

We soon ran out of drinks, and my business partner went to the corner shop to purchase more. When he came back, he looked wild-eyed and announced: "D'you know that this building is on fire?"

Even in his sober moments, my partner loved adrenaline-pumpers. Since he appeared more excited than alarmed, we at first put it down to his having had a few too many. Then I drew the curtains to the picture window facing the high street.

Foggy-eyed, I whistled in amazement. At least seven fire engines, ambulances, and all kinds of firefighting paraphernalia were right there on our street.

I had no idea at the time, but for me this fire was a waking dream from the Holy Spirit, telling me about my near future.

Second Fire

The second waking dream of fire took place in the United States while I was attending the Rotary International Convention in Kansas City, Missouri.

My wife was pregnant then, and she tired easily. During break time, we retired to our hotel, which was close to the convention center. We were hardly asleep, when the doorbell rang. I opened the door and found myself faced by a young American firefighter in full battle dress.

"You must evacuate at once!" he said, smiling gently when he saw my wife's frightened face. "There is a fire in the basement."

Third Fire

The third fire occurred in India.

I had just returned from the Nigerian High Commission in New Delhi around ten o'clock and was preparing for bed in my hotel room. Just as I began to compose myself to sleep, I heard some commotion outside.

"They call this a five-star hotel?" I asked in disgust as the noise outside the hotel room grew.

When I opened the door to investigate, someone shouted, "There's another one here!"

"Another what?" I asked stupidly.

I was informed that there was a fire in the linen store on this very floor, the sixth. Apparently, everybody else on this floor had learned of the fire and had evacuated.

Perhaps this was the Holy Spirit's way of telling me that my house was already on fire, yet I was the last to know!

Party's Over

When I started my business, back in late 1979, I had no closing hour. My closing hour was whenever the work that a client needed next day was completed. I was architect, engineer, accountant, draftsman, and quantity surveyor—and sometimes even estate surveyor and typist—rolled into one. I had put my very heart into that business.

When the business began to prosper in 1982, I took on partners. This partnership would be a source of strength, but also an Achilles' heel.

A military coup on the closing day of 1983 changed the business terrain dramatically. Many of my patrons in government were suddenly out of power.

I had confidence that the future was still good for a company that was built on more than hype and patronage, but some of my colleagues began to view the horizon with apprehension. Later, their apprehension turned into action. They didn't just take a walk; they disemboweled the company in my absence, carting away its most important assets—hardware and project files.

There had been no formal partnership agreement. I had operated on good faith, as had my former bosses. So there was little material to go on in the way of litigation. Yet, my property was the sole guarantor of all financial transactions with the banks.

This, I thought, was as good a time as any to let God be the judge. It was my first poignant lesson on surrender.

A pall of negativity shrouded the affairs of the company. Efforts to revive it were like trying to find one's way out of a black hole.

Banks love winners and are nervous about losers. And in this case, I was the loser. They only knew me as the loan and overdraft guarantor. Formerly eager to lend money amidst oily banter, smiles, and pumping handshakes—at a time we hardly needed the money—the banks now moved in like vultures on a carcass in the savanna.

At one point, only a court order that arrived not a minute too soon saved my property from being auctioned at a ridiculous price to cover a small part of our liabilities.

Into Exile

At this point, my marriage also became shaky. To keep my sanity and the respect of our children, I relocated to my hometown, an hour's drive away. It was a unilateral trial separation that went all the way eventually.

In the state capital where I'd been living, I had been landlord of two large residences. Back in my hometown, all I could afford was a two-room flat. I would stay there for two years with four of my kids—three girls and one boy—who followed me into "exile."

I used to be busy. Now I had time to read even old newspapers—sometimes twice.

What Would Come Next?

Had I been aware, I would have seen the waking-dream symbol about the near future: it was as good a time as any to start reading the records of my past lives to see where I'd been and find a new direction.

I was yet to be aware of it, but I had arrived at that moment in my dream worlds where I was stuck on a broken staircase with no door to enter and no stairs to descend back to familiar ground.

The Learjet dream—a symbol of material wealth—was long gone. What would come next?

When it came time for local-government elections, I thought running for office might be the secret door to a new life. But the political "landlords" of this terrain thought otherwise. They swarmed me like hornets, using meaner tactics than I could ever have imagined, coming from the staid background of architecture. I was shot down like a guinea fowl in flight.

So much for politics—at least for that time.

It was at this crossroads in my life that an old school friend named Harold—strange name for a Nigerian—who lived in Lagos invited me to spend a weekend in his Ikeja residence.

This was yet another waking dream, had I the awareness to see it.

I had never heard of Eckankar then, much less known that the spiritual leader's first name was Harold. When the Lagos Harold invited me to his residence, another Harold would invite me for a different trip—into the God worlds!

Try this spiritual exercise today!

Show Me Love

If you don't know anything about ECK, the main tool you have to work with at this point may be prayer—your communication with God. If you are sincerely interested in truth, in knowing who you are and why you belong here, ask God in your prayers: "Show me truth."

If your heart is pure, the Lord will bring truth into your life. But don't expect it to come in a way that fits your expectations; it may come in a different way. It may come through the gift of a book or by way of a person telling you one small step that you need to take before you can go to the next step.

And so you can pray to God. Just say, "I want truth," or "Dear Lord, give me knowledge, wisdom, and understanding." But the greatest thing you could ask is: "Dear Lord, give me love."

Knowledge, wisdom, and understanding are only the attributes of God. But when you have love, you have the whole thing. We seek first the highest, most divine, most sacred part of something which is nothing other than our own inner being. And with this come the attributes of God and the spiritual liberation, which is something no baptism can ever bring.

When you ask for truth with a pure heart, Divine Spirit will take you one step closer to coming home to God.

—Sri Harold Klemp
The Spiritual Exercises of ECK[3]

2

Face-to-Face

There is one way to know the Living ECK Master is authentic. That is to see him on some higher plane where assumption is impossible. If the Mahanta is seen in his radiant form, the chela knows this is the true Master of Eckankar. It is only when the chela is ready that he will see the Mahanta in the radiant form.

—*The Shariyat-Ki-Sugmad*, Books One & Two[1]

When I arrived in Lagos, my friend Harold and I began to debrief each other fully about what had happened since we last met a few years back.

Weekend in Lagos

At bedtime, we took the guest bedroom and planned to continue our conversation till the fog of sleep overtook one or both of us.

Toward daybreak, I came awake in the world of dreams! The clarity of my experiences in that dream was better than here in the physical world. I never wrote it down, since dreams were not important to me yet, but the details of that experience were permanently burned on my mind.

Awake in the World of Dreams

I found myself at what I thought to be the National Stadium in Surulere, Lagos, in company of many others. A marketplace murmur hung around us as we waited. Then, for no apparent reason, the crowd began to scream!

What are they screaming about? I wondered, more curious than alarmed.

Get outside! An inner impression barked.

It occurred to me that "outside" lay at the end of a long arcade that started from where we stood. I began the long, brisk walk to the end of the arcade alone.

The further I walked from the starting point, the louder the sound became. By the time I got midway to my destination, the sound had turned into something like several jet fighters screaming down a runway to take off.

Once I made the exit, the jet planes seemed to have taken off. The sound of their engines diminished in a few seconds. The megadecibels dropped to absolute zero, making me wonder, *Which was louder, the sound or the silence?*

This Is Not Lagos

My first thought "outside" was: *This is not Lagos!*

I had emerged in a countryside that reminded me of central Nigeria, my home.

A low hill stood close by, with only grass and no trees on top. In the distance, blue hills that reminded me of the mountain range that separates Nigeria and Cameroon stood sentry.

A brassy midmorning sunlight bathed the countryside, but the sun that gave rise to it was not in evidence. And strangely, even though the sunlight was brilliant and brassy, it was neither hot nor cold.

Why am I here? I thought.

Look up! an inner voice barked once again.

In later years, I would identify this voice as that of ECK Master Rebazar Tarzs.

My eyes turned skyward.

A beam of light came as if from a distant lighthouse in the deep recesses of the sky. It began to spiral down funnel-like from its source. The hilltops were the first to receive the light, then the few scattered trees, grasses, and finally the earth at my feet.

Everything this light fell upon—which was virtually the whole countryside in which I stood—was transformed. From the ordinary, everything took on the purest white translucence. Every shadow was banished from the landscape!

Who can beat that? I thought, fascinated.

Look up! that inner voice barked once more.

Another pinpoint of light started from where the first one had come. Instead of funneling itself down, it came like a lantern, a single unit. And it traveled more rapidly. Very soon it arrived and suspended itself about waist-high and five steps away from where I stood.

I looked with curiosity at this new arrival.

This Fellow Interests Me

On a piece of cloud the size of a Muslim prayer rug, a man sat in the classic yogi style, his legs folded under him and his back ramrod straight. He fixed me with an unblinking stare, and I looked back curiously at him.

He had Caucasian features, an aquiline nose, and a slightly receding hairline. He struck me as sharp and dynamic, though he didn't move a muscle or say anything. And he was slim, perhaps even thin. His cloud seat seemed to be made of the purest cumulus cloud or combed cotton. His translucent body looked like millions of live fireflies twinkled inside him. I was curious, and I noticed something: He could cast a shadow here when nothing else could. However, when I took a step toward his cloud throne to find out why he could cast a shadow here when even I couldn't, he disappeared—along with the whole countryside!

I woke up as clearheaded as if I had just come from a morning walk in the garden. Yet what I said next surprised even me.

"Would you believe it if I said I'd just been to heaven and back?" I was talking to my friend Harold, who had also just woken up.

"And did you see me there?" Harold asked me, as if he'd been waiting for that question.

What was taking place was Golden-tongued Wisdom. But I did not recognize it then.

Harold of Ikeja was actually asking me, in the language of prophecy, *When you went to heaven, did you see Harold—my namesake—there?* Meaning Sri Harold Klemp, the Mahanta, the Living ECK Master, spiritual leader of Eckankar.

Darshan

Much later, in my study of the ECK works, I learned the name of an experience such as I had—the Darshan, the meeting with the Mahanta. *The Shariyat-Ki-Sugmad* says,

No one ever comes to the Mahanta, the Living ECK Master until his good karma brings him. . . . Their good karma is not utilized to purchase worldly position and wealth, but applied to secure something vastly more important; that is, the Darshan, the meeting with the Living ECK Master. They come to him with a love, a capacity to love, an inheritance which has brought them directly to the feet of the Living ECK Master.[2]

Furthermore, I was given secrets of the universes of God that night.

The Light and Sound that banished all shadows was the ECK, the Holy Spirit and Voice of God. "Mr. Fireflies" was the Mahanta. The reason the Mahanta cast a shadow was because he was the only real thing in that land.

No one ever considered me a spiritual person. And that "no one" included myself. But after this experience, I began to have a powerful hunger for God.

At first, though, I felt embarrassed. Me, having a hunger for God?

Hunger for God

Much of what I had seen of organized religion, right from missionary-school days, had put me off.

In our American missionary-run secondary school, I saw lots of students who paid lip service to religion to please the school authorities. This pretense was often mistaken for piety, and I had little use for that sham.

But I now had this longing for God that I couldn't wish away.

You've got to do something about this tenderness for God, the inner yearning said.

But how?

At one time, I thought that if I had the money, I would construct a pyramid in my residence—a place where I could retire for an hour or so each day. I later realized this was an unconscious memory from ancient

Egypt. In hindsight, I thank God I had no such money to waste. But perhaps this was a foreshadowing of my spiritual search.

After my dream meeting with the Mahanta, I spent a whole year of searching for a spiritual path, but nothing turned up. At this time, I decided to team up with a branch of Christianity that I had never explored in this life before—Catholicism.

Searching

What I thought was just a spontaneous idea turned out to be karma driven. I had an old debt to settle in the Catholic Church.

The Protestant clergy and laity always, from my point of view, put themselves apart from life around them, while the Catholics seemed to embrace life with gusto. Some might even say too much gusto.

Anyhow, at this time, I considered Catholics less prone to the "us versus them" that I had found in the Protestant church of my youth. I had no intention of cutting myself off from life just because I was following God.

Even at that time, I suspected that God and life were not antithetical to each other.

Perhaps after going through a few Catholic mysteries, I would somehow come face-to-face with what I was looking for spiritually inside. And I did—but not as they or I had planned.

One day I, the fresh convert, walked into the residence of a parish priest."Is there a specific thing I can do to help out in your parish?" I asked.

The priest adjusted his glasses on his nose and took a long look at me—the way a scientist might look at a new, hard-to-classify specimen. He was more used to parishioners looking to be served than to serve.

The Rosary

We had a long discussion, and the priest was so pleased with his new catch that he blessed a rosary and gave it to me as a gift of love.

What a surprise it would be to this priest if he were to learn what followed. For with the gift of that rosary, he had inadvertently started me on the path that would lead me into the heart of Eckankar.

Rain or shine, traveling or stationary, I would recite the rosary promptly at six o'clock, without missing a day. I went at it as if my life depended on it, for perhaps a year.

If I was alone—whether in my bedroom or out driving—I would recite the rosary aloud while fingering the beads.

When I had company, such as in a bus or taxi, or was in the presence of others, I would recite the rosary silently, counting the prayers off with my fingers. My intentions were to break through into the Catholic mysteries, not to make a show of piety.

I never broke through into the Catholic mysteries with the rosary, but there was one useful achievement I got for my efforts. I developed a focus in my inner life and regularity in my spiritual practices. This discipline would prove useful later, when I found the teachings of Eckankar.

When I first found Eckankar, the spiritual exercises would gobble up four months of untiring, inflexible devotion—twenty minutes or more each time, twice a day, without results—before I struck gold!

Paul Twitchell's Books

Paul Twitchell's books were my first contact with Eckankar. When I first read them, they changed my life. I had never read anything like this in scripture. And my introduction to Paul's books is a story in itself.

"Why do humans find it impossible to live at peace with each other?" I threw this question partly to the air around me, expecting no real plausible answer.

"That's how God intended it!" said my friend Joe— the man I had gone to look for in Kaduna years before.

I thought I misheard him.

He had left a small shortwave radio on for entertainment as he worked on a metal-tinkering project. The radio was blaring out the latest news about forces led by the United States that had gathered in the Middle East to drive out the invading Iraqi forces from Kuwait.

I looked at Joe's face for a clever smirk or some sign of a tongue-in-cheek remark. *He must be pulling my leg*, I thought.

But apparently, he wasn't.

Method to the Madness

My mind went back along memory lane to missionary school. Christianity had drummed into us ancient stories of a raging war between God and Satan. The world would have remained perfect and peaceful—as God intended—if not for Satan, who had a different agenda from God's.

But here my friend Joe was telling me that God not only foresaw the chaos, but He'd planned for it in creation ab initio!

I imagined our old pastor hearing this. Strange as it might sound, that "blasphemy" provided a ray of hope for me.

I had been steadily losing respect for a God that created everything and yet refused to take responsibility for its resulting chaos. If Satan were the problem he is made out to be, why did God not destroy Satan?

We Are Here to Learn to Love

"To what purpose did God plan for and foresee chaos?" I asked Joe.

"So that you and I and everybody could be trained—trained to love!" he said.

Joe continued, "Chaos is a quicker teacher than, say, peace and comfort. Who needs God when the stomach is full and there's money in the bank and no illness or death threatens?"

"Where did you get all this from?" I asked, since I knew he did not get it from our common religious background.

Instead of long talk, he gave me a book. Its title was *The Flute of God*, and the author was Paul Twitchell.

Never heard of him, I thought. But I went home and read the book anyway.

I had had enough of people thrusting their scriptures at me—challenging me if I dared question them or condemning me if I didn't believe them even before we started a discussion.

Paul Twitchell let his conclusions stand, or fall, with the reader's experience. If he referred to any scriptures, it was to take the reader from what was already familiar to what Paul was trying to show: how life and spirituality lock into and support each other.

Life Is a Religion We Were All Born Into!

The startling and exciting understanding I got from Paul Twitchell's book was that life is a religion we were all born into. It is a combination of the good, the bad, and the everything, and that's fine! If I were to become an ECKist, it was not something new or different I was going into. Since ECK (Divine Spirit) is life itself, I was already in it! The only problem was, I had never thought of it as a religion.

Paul was barking up my tree!

In *The Flute of God* he devoted an entire chapter to "The Unknown Name of God." He said that singing the word *HU*, silently or aloud, could attune us to Divine Spirit and enhance our spiritual understanding of life.

I sang HU in an unbroken routine for four months, without result. Then, toward the end of May 1991, I had this powerful inner nudge to begin recording my dreams.

Dream Journal

I bought a big loose-leaf binder and put paper in it. I would log my dreams from now on.

On May 31, I captured my first dream.

Two vehicles are lined up behind my Santana saloon car (sedan). Nearest is a thirty-seater commuter bus. Behind the bus stands a large articulated lorry (semitrailer). A powerful silver chain connects all three vehicles, rear bumper to front bumper.

"The batteries of these vehicles are cold," I hear someone say via the inner channels. "They need to be jumpstarted."

Immediately, a hook from a mobile crane grips the front bumper of the Santana and begins to tow it. Because of the silver chain, all three vehicles begin to move faster and faster.

When the engines finally cough into life, all three vehicles burst into flames.

I didn't understand this dream right away. But after diligently recording my dreams over time, I built my own dream dictionary. At this point, I could decipher the symbols and so understand the dream.

Jump Started

The saloon car (sedan) represented my physical body; the bus was the Astral body, the seat of emotions; and the articulated lorry (semitrailer) represented the Causal (memory) body, which contains the seeds of karma and records of our incarnations in these lower worlds.

The strong silver-colored chain represented the silver cord, the element that hooks these bodies together. This silver cord is severed at the death of the physical body.

I was to discover later in my study of dreams that the last time I worked directly with a Living ECK Master, like I am doing at present, was about three and a half centuries ago. No wonder the batteries were cold!

The four months of spiritual exercises had been warming up things in the spiritual fireplace, but I didn't know this yet.

Two days after my cold-batteries dream, I began to have proof that Paul Twitchell was speaking truth.

Out of the Body

A joyous current of energy coursed through my body on the night of June 2 and morning of June 3, 1991. While doing a spiritual exercise, this current had started cascading into me from somewhere above. It was an incredible current of blessedness. And it did not stop even when I had finished doing the spiritual exercise!

Current of Energy

The children had left for school, and my wife returned to bed after preparing breakfast. I did my physical exercises and tried to relax. It was no use.

This current of energy poured relentlessly into me from that invisible source. I soon began to feel like a sixty-watt lightbulb that was now compelled to carry a thousand watts. I was in a state of tremendous joy, but I could not relax. I couldn't do anything but fidget. What could I do to get rid of this excess energy?

The worst part of all was that I couldn't share this with my wife, since I had kept these spiritual exercises to myself. It was my way of not imposing on her spiritually. She did become an ECKist later, but it was at her own volition.

I went into the family lounge and lay supine on the couch, hoping to cool off. In a few moments, I drifted into that twilight zone where sleep and wakefulness meet. Then a sound started in one of my ears.

I cannot recall which ear; I just recall it was in only one ear, though there was nothing wrong with the other ear.

The sound was like that of a chain grating over the teeth of a sprocket.

When I tried to lift my hand, it did not move. Then, as the sound got louder, I found myself being slowly lifted clear of the couch!

Was I Levitating?

Instead of being frightened, I found it exhilarating. Was I levitating?

I soon discovered I wasn't. The body that was rising above the couch was not the physical body; it was a light transparent body. And the higher this body went, the more light and joy and wisdom I acquired, and the louder was the sound! This rising body was lying horizontally in the supine position, just like the physical one on the couch.

When I reached the ceiling and my nose, toes, and

perhaps lips began to penetrate through the ceiling, the sound stopped. Once the sound stopped, the upward movement also halted.

What now?

After a few minutes, I began to hear the sound of sweeping. And the sound was coming toward the door to the lounge. I realized it was our steward, someone we employed to help with household chores since my wife tired easily.

He had resumed work around eight o'clock and was now sweeping the passage that led into the lounge.

In my suspended position, I had been happy and without a care in the world. I was wiser and happier, and I felt lighter. Things I had never known before, I now knew. I did not have to turn to look at anything, as I had vision wherever I needed it. But now that sound of sweeping gave me worries.

Snapped Back

Had I come into the lounge to do a spiritual exercise, I would have locked the door. But I hadn't. And I knew that this body that had penetrated halfway into the ceiling was no good for locking doors.

My predicament is funny in hindsight. I thought someone coming into the room would see both the body sniffing the ceiling and the physical one on the settee. I knew exactly what the steward would do upon seeing such a phenomenon: He would run screaming from the room. This would bring the neighbors, and I might have to answer awkward questions.

I didn't know that the body I was now in was not visible to the human eye.

As the sound of sweeping got close to the door, my panic caused the body on the ceiling to snap back into the one on the couch. Immediately, I lost all my newly acquired powers of 360-degree vision and all the knowledge that came without effort or thought—and also much of the joy and lightness.

I found this rather sad. But there was an upside to it all: I had lost a chunk of my fear of death. I had just discovered that I did not need the physical body to be alive! In fact, I fared better in some ways without it. I would still not be in any hurry to leave my physical body permanently, but from that time on I was no longer so desperately attached to it.

How Do You Know I Exist?

The teachings of Eckankar say the Mahanta, the Living ECK Master is spiritually with his chelas (spiritual students, or disciples) at all times.

How do you know I exist? I had often wondered. How can the Master say he is always with me when he is over ten thousand kilometers (six thousand miles) away in the United States of America? The constant presence of the Master did not make sense.

But a week or so after the out-of-body experience just related, I had another one. The Master would answer my question in a most startling manner.

At ten o'clock that night, I sat down to do a spiritual exercise. I sang HU for twenty to thirty minutes. Then I went into quiet contemplation for some time. When I was about to end it, I got an inner nudge to continue.

Singularity

I must have sat like this for thirty minutes or more. Then, suddenly, my vision and total attention zoomed in like a camera lens to a singularity with the pulling power of a black hole! Pictures and images that had been flashing intermittently on the screen of my inner vision all disappeared, leaving a blank blue-gray screen. Concentrating was now no problem. As a matter of fact, shifting my attention away from this singularity was now the problem!

I could no longer feel the bite of mosquitoes nor any itch or disturbance to my body. It felt as if my total being had compressed to this single point. I had, for the first time, accessed the "blank screen" which Paul Twitchell had written about.

Unable to remove my attention from this screen, I sat and waited.

Suddenly, this singularity I seemed to have turned into began to expand outward.

Expanded Viewpoint

I expanded, and I soon filled the whole room. Once I filled the room, the expansion halted very briefly. In those few seconds of halted expansion, I seemed to turn into a single eyeball! And then the eyeball began to expand beyond the confines of the living room.

The expansion now became very fast. In perhaps less than a minute, the eyeball had expanded and attained oneness with the globe of our Earth. I was now planet Earth, and yet I also now watched myself as if from a satellite in space.

My attention turned to my surface.

New York Swam into View

The oceans came into view like on a toy globe that a child could hold in his hands. Huge, silver-colored ocean liners were chugging across the oceans, throwing white foam as they moved from one continent to another.

I have never been to New York in this life except for a brief stop to change planes at the John F. Kennedy International Airport. But I was born there in my last life, and perhaps because of this, New York now swam into my memory; and the city itself immediately came into view. It was the lower Manhattan area. I could focus my vision like a zoom lens if I wanted more detail. My body was sitting on a couch in central Nigeria, but I could have read the license plate of a car on the streets of New York if I had chosen to!

Whether my attention turned to Moscow or any other place on Earth, the place would simply swim into perfect focus.

All I Needed to Be Aware

I was not limited to distant big scenes only. All I needed to be aware of something was to consider or think of it, and it was there before me.

My neighbor's dogs were very agitated, so I turned my attention there to find out what was ailing them. Then my attention turned to the crickets beating their wings under the fluorescent security light below my northern window. I was immediately in communication with them.

"Wow!" I marveled.

I stayed like this awhile, wishing it would go on forever. But sadly, my viewpoint began to shrink in the reverse order that it had expanded. Soon I was back in my room and in my body—an ordinary human being only aware within the four corners of the room.

"What was all that about?" I asked the Mahanta.

Suddenly I knew! It was in answer to my question "How do you know I exist?"

Face-to-Face

Around April 1991, I had heard through the grapevine that the Living ECK Master, the spiritual leader of Eckankar who had inherited Paul Twitchell's mantle, would be present at the 1991 ECK African Seminar, to be held in Lagos sometime in July. I would simply *have* to be there. I needed to see this fellow face-to-face in order to make up my mind about a whole lot of things.

Two weeks before the seminar, I met my first obstacle: I became hopelessly broke. To compound that problem, I had a close friend who wanted to make the trip with me—at my expense! This friend had once read the ECK books I had borrowed just to find something in them to ridicule. But he was now sincerely interested and wanted to go to Lagos to check out the modern prophet, the Living ECK Master. However, his money situation was worse than mine.

Ten- to Twelve-Hour Journey

My plan to fly into Lagos with my wife, who was six months pregnant, was now definitely out the window. The ten- to twelve-hour overland journey that had been unthinkable at first was now the only option if I wanted to attend the seminar.

I finally scraped up enough money to hire a taxi that would take all three of us to Lagos. A friend in Lagos had graciously agreed to accommodate us in his servants' quarters. It was not a trip for the proud.

Since the taxi driver was even less familiar with Lagos than we were, we arrived an hour before midnight and then missed a couple of turns, which prolonged our journey to the suburb of Ikoyi for another two hours or so. At the time, I had no idea, but such events can be par for the course when one starts on a journey to meet the spiritual leader of Eckankar.

Largest ECK Seminar

ECKists who attended the 1991 ECK African Seminar will not forget it in a hurry. It was my first ECK seminar ever. And it was by far the largest ECK seminar that had ever taken place.[3]

In fact, the turnout was so unexpectedly large that space at the venue became a huge problem.

The main auditorium at the National Theatre Lagos, where the seminar took place, was designed to seat only five thousand people. More than ten thousand turned up, and each person wanted to be in that hall to witness the modern-day prophet in the flesh!

Ushers and crowd control proved inadequate for the multitude. The surging crowd knocked the guardians at the gates aside like ninepins! The hall was full, yet the colossal black python of human bodies kept snaking its way into that main hall of the National Theatre.

Long after the event was over, I wondered why a disaster of unimaginable proportion had not taken place. I was yet to become aware of the mysterious ways of the Holy Spirit acting through Its chief agent, the Mahanta, the Living ECK Master.

The three of us (wife, friend, and I) found seats, courtesy of my metal-tinkering friend Joe. He had been in the hall earlier for a meeting of registered students of Eckankar. I could not attend because my registration was yet to come through.

We got in and immediately squeezed into the reserved seats an hour before the Master's appearance. But our struggle in getting to those seats was child's play compared to what people had to go through about an hour later.

Overcrowded Hall

Near where I sat, a column of front-runners crashed through the wall of ushers and crowd controllers who were yelling, without effect, that the hall was now overfilled. The ushers were like mere gnats before a charge of elephants.

Now with nowhere to sit and nowhere to move, those in front of the surging crowd stood squashed against a flimsy aluminum balcony railing that danced under pressure like the legs of mosquitoes carrying cement. That balcony railing was the only barrier between these front-runners and the abyss of the main seating bowl below!

Meanwhile, those outside were incessantly pushing to get in, unaware there was nowhere for those in front of them to go—unless the balcony railing broke under pressure. Then those being crushed against it would spill over onto the heads of those in the main seating bowl far below—many of whom were sitting on the floor, since the seats had long been filled.

I winced every time the incoming crowd pushed. Many people were shouting, others were groaning, and others even sounded as if they were crying from being so squeezed. Yet people outside continually pushed from behind to get into the hall.

It is said that a million angels can dance on the head of a pin. But here we were facing the nitty-gritty of physical reality, which says that only so many people can be squeezed into so much space.

That the flimsy balcony railing held and the crowd leaning on it did not spill two stories down onto the heads of those in the overcrowded hall below was actually the first miracle I witnessed at an ECK function.

Greeting the Master

The MC soon led us in a HU song. It was perhaps the first time I had heard a group HU song.

Ten thousand voices sang and hummed like a million bees droning in the sunshine. I could not even hear my own voice!

"Ladies and gentlemen," the MC announced, "Sri Harold Klemp, the Mahanta, the Living ECK Master!"

I opened my eyes, anticipating the wonder of finally seeing what the Master, Sri Harold Klemp—whose name I had just discovered at this seminar—looked like.

This fellow is harmless! was my first impression. An ordinary-looking white man who exuded no obvious power, pomp, or authority graced the stage. Nearby sat the French-language interpreter.

Sri Harold could have been mistaken for a carefully dressed, conservative businessman. He wore no religious garb, but a simple blue jacket, shirt, and striped tie. He sat carefully, crossing one leg over the other. His black shoes were well polished, and his hair was neatly brushed.

Compared to the clergy we are used to seeing in the religions around us, sometimes dressed to thrill, Sri Harold looked too ordinary and down-to-earth to be a spiritual leader whose blessings reach millions and who appears routinely in countless people's dreams and contemplations.

He toyed with the microphone cord as he began to speak.

A Modern Prophet Speaks

"In a crowd this size, we must be more careful and full of love than usual," he said. Strangely enough, the crowd began to respond.

The cries from those in the front of the balcony—still pressed against the flimsy aluminum railing that threatened to give way any moment—began to recede. It was obvious that the incessant pressure from behind was easing up.

Once the pressure began to ease off and the thunderous applause had died down enough, the Master continued to speak in very slow American English. I believe it was in deference to the audience that spoke

English as a second or even third language. The title of his talk was *A Better Friend of the Mahanta*. He related simple stories that he said would be easier to remember, and he encouraged us to take them into contemplation at home to find their whole meaning.

Blue Light

While the Mahanta, the Living ECK Master spoke, I closed my eyes and looked toward the stage with the inner spiritual vision.

At home, when I contemplated with eyes closed, the Blue Light of the Mahanta would come in a swirling motion that waxed and waned like waves lapping the shoreline. Sometimes the Light whirled like the rotors of helicopter blades. But this time, what I witnessed in my Spiritual Eye was a solid, unmoving, and unpulsing sheet of medium-blue light. No swirling, no waxing or waning. Perhaps it was because Sri Harold, as both the Outer and Inner Master, was present in the room.

Singing HU with the Audience

At the end of his talk, Sri Harold sang HU with the audience. I would not discover the immense significance of this action till years later.

I opened my eyes to watch the Master go. Would he just dissolve like mist from the stage, or would he walk away like an ordinary human being?

The crowd went on singing HU. Sri Harold stopped, placed the microphone carefully on the table, and got up, looking to make sure he did not trip on the microphone cable. As he walked off stage, I observed that he was slim, perhaps even thin—like "Mr. Fireflies" in my dream two years back on that memorable weekend in Lagos. The only difference was that his body was not transparent out here, nor did it sparkle like fireflies. But my mind still questioned:

Was this really "Mr. Fireflies" of two years back?

Outside the National Theatre, events were already cooking to answer that question.

Spiritual and Sports History

As spiritual history was going on in the National Theatre, sports history was also being made at the National Stadium in Lagos, the symbolic venue of my dream experience two years back.

The Nigerian national football team, the Green Eagles, were up against the Stallions of Burkina Faso for a FIFA-organized competition. It was the Eagle against the Horse, the swift ruler of the air against that of the earth—the spiritual versus the material. Who would win?

The Eagle walloped the Horse seven goals to one. Symbolically, for every HU Sri Harold sang inside the theater, the Nigerian national team scored a goal! Some would put it down to coincidence, but I would mull over the significance of this event for a long time. Was this victory a symbol of the spiritual finally being able, through love—the song of HU—to defeat the downward pull of materialism in our spiritual lives?

I can't recall, in the history of this country, a more decisive victory of the national team against a visiting team in a FIFA-organized match at that venue.

Homeward Bound

After we had seen the Master, we headed back to Ikoyi.

A visitor had parked a red Honda Prelude in the driveway of our hosts' residence. I did not know it yet, but this would be the first step in reconnecting with the spiritual dream experience I'd had two years earlier on that weekend in Lagos visiting my friend Harold, who lived in the suburb of Ikeja.

It was Harold of Ikeja's wife visiting our host family at Ikoyi. She let me know that her husband was in town. She added that she was sure he would be happy to welcome us at their Ikeja residence.

Our road out of Lagos passed through Ikeja, and I thought it would be a good idea to get a jump on the Lagos traffic gridlock in the morning. So we bade our Ikoyi host family good-bye and followed the red Prelude to Ikeja. *At least we can afford a one-day stay at a reasonably priced motel in Ikeja,* I thought.

Yet to Be Impressed

At the time, I was yet to be impressed by the significance of this turn of events.

Two years ago, I'd had that vivid spiritual experience with "Mr. Fireflies" in the residence of Harold of Ikeja, in Lagos. Today, after I met a different Harold at the National Theatre, I never gave a thought to my host of two years ago, much less consider visiting him. Yet here I was, on my way to reconnect with the Harold in whose house the first experience—which could have been with the Harold I met today at the National Theatre—occurred!

After the pleasantries and dinner at Ikeja, we asked to be shown to a reasonably priced motel.

To the Very Same Room

"Your friend and the taxi driver will be shown to a motel," Harold said. "But for you and your wife, I have a place—if you would accept it." Then he showed us to the very room where, two years ago, I had met "Mr. Fireflies" in the dream state!

Yet, all this seemed routine at the time. It would take a couple of years for me to become impressed with the spiritual meaning of this "coincidence."

I noticed two peculiar things immediately after listening to the Mahanta speak at the National Theatre. For one thing, my face burned and flushed. It was like what had happened once when I climbed above the clouds to the top of Mount Kilimanjaro in Tanzania. The second thing I noticed was my initial inability to fall asleep that night.

I normally have no problem falling asleep, even under the worst conditions. But today, I was experiencing just that—I was unable to drop off to sleep. It felt like the agitation that preceded my first Soul Travel experience. However, I finally fell asleep around half past four in the morning.

Meeting an Old Friend

In the dream state, the Mahanta appeared once more.

I found myself at his doorstep. In the dream, he was an old friend. I was planning to return to Makurdi— the place I had left when my company failed. This friend was to help me return and settle down after my long sojourn from Makurdi, the state capital. This was symbolic of Soul returning home into the worlds beyond time and space, a place It had left eons ago.

As I was about to knock on the door, a drama ensued nearby. This drama symbolized my original descent, as Soul, into the lower worlds of time and space. I had not exactly come flying first-class, but more like a frightened chick caught in the talons of a hawk.

A hawk swoops out of the skies and into a fire-scorched field of Guinea corn nearby.

When the hawk takes to the air once more, it holds in its talons a chick, chirping piteously. I can't believe the level of grief and helplessness that washes over me as that hawk carries away its prize over the horizon.

I still hold the doorknob, waiting for God-knows-what. But as I wait, a speck appears over the horizon from where the hawk had disappeared, and I watch it approach.

It's the hawk, and as it flies overhead, I notice that it now carries a beautiful young woman who cradles a child lovingly in her arms. They are laughing and so happy—a complete contrast to the frightened chicken that had been borne away.

Soul's Journey

I had left the higher worlds of Divine Spirit like an unwilling, frightened chicken caught in the talons of a hawk. Guinea corn, being the last crop to be harvested in my area, indicated that I had been a straggler—among the last in my "batch" to be ready for harvest. My spiritual "age mates"—those Souls who came to the lower worlds with me—had since all returned home, as the Master told me years later.

One night, many years after this experience, I asked the Mahanta just how long I had been loitering in the lower worlds of time and space.

"Thirty-five million years since the first man!" was the curt reply.

In contemplation, I felt staggered. *Thirty-five million years!* And that did not include the incarnations lower than the human form. I was not exactly a spiritual spring chicken! No wonder my graves in the lower worlds, in my childhood dream experiences, had stretched from horizon to horizon.

When I tell someone about Eckankar and they look blank, I understand. It took me thirty-five million years to come to this moment!

Next day, I headed back home to Gboko—and to a new life. Thirty-five days later, my brand-new Eckankar

ID card and *The ECK Dream Discourses* arrived in the mailbox. After thirty-five million years in this land ruled by the Angel of Death with an inflexible, merciless hand, my spiritual journey home had commenced!

Try this spiritual exercise today!

Consultation with the Master

Visualize yourself sitting in a large room, waiting for a consultation with the Mahanta.* As you wait, look about the room. Note the furniture you're sitting in and other pieces about you. There are several ECKists around you that you may recognize and chat with a bit before you are told that you can go in.

The door opens, and you see yourself go into the inner room and meet the Mahanta. You have about fifteen or twenty minutes to talk about whatever you want, before a knock will come on the door to signal that you have a few more minutes to wrap it up. Then the door will open, and someone will say, "It's been nice you could be here," and escort you out. Another person is then led into the room.

By practicing this exercise, you can arrange this private time to meet with the Mahanta on the inner planes.

—Sri Harold Klemp
The Spiritual Exercises of ECK[4]

* The Mahanta, the Living ECK Master is the spiritual leader of Eckankar and the inner guide for ECKists (followers of Eckankar). Members of other religions can adapt this spiritual exercise for whomever they look to as a spiritual guide.

Part Two

Travels from Earth into the Heavens

3

Spiritual Matriculation

He who enters into the works of Eckankar becomes an Acolyte. He is put under the spiritual discipline of ECK, prior to his true induction into the invisible order. He is a probationer who must prove his worth before entering into the true works of Eckankar.

—The Shariyat-Ki-Sugmad, Books One & Two[1]

When I found the teachings of Eckankar, I had to move beyond faith to experience. It seemed like a big, insurmountable gap existed between the two. One evening, a young man demonstrated just how big that gap could be for lots of people.

The just shall live by faith, the scriptures of traditional religions often say. But how many can dare let experience abrogate, adjust, or confirm their faith?

Better (Not Just) Believe It!

As a friend and I were chatting in front of his office, a well-dressed young man stopped in front of us and, without our permission, opened a large, floppy, dog-eared Bible and began to preach to us from it.

We listened to him patiently till he paused to catch his breath. When I asked, he confirmed that he was just getting off work. Preaching the "good news" came before a good meal and rest, apparently. There must be a great reward or incentive to inspire such dedication. So I inquired about that.

"As a man of faith," he said, standing tall, "I hope to go to heaven when I die."

"Have you ever been there, by any chance, to confirm whether heaven is worth all this effort?" I asked him.

He avoided a yes-or-no answer, like a witness in court trying to avoid a lawyer's unfairly loaded question. To answer with a straight yes or no, he would either look bad or be forced to lie.

"I *hope* to be there," he repeated dully, wondering at this line of questioning.

In his world, there were believers and nonbelievers. Each had a final place in eternity to match his belief or unbelief. *What is there to question?* he seemed to be wondering.

"Well, I've been there, and I am ready to share my experience," I said, breaking the news to him.

I would have given a lot to know why he reacted the way he did. But he never gave me the chance.

Why Didn't He Ask?

The fellow jumped back a couple of feet from me as if he had seen a cobra! Without another word, he closed his floppy Bible and retreated almost at a trot, not even glancing back, as if he wanted to put the greatest distance between us in the shortest possible time. He then crossed the road and went into the gathering night market.

Strange reaction from a man who was working so hard to get to heaven and found someone who claimed to have been there.

Why didn't he ask how I got there and what the place looked like? I wondered.

But perhaps I knew the answer, because I had been in his position before I found the teachings of Eckankar. Faith and experience had fought each other almost to a standstill till the Master intervened.

From Faith to Experience

All the time I had been reading *The Flute of God*, by the modern-day founder of Eckankar, Paul Twitchell, I thought Eckankar was a faith-based religion like all others. What I read, I believed. What I didn't believe went out the window—kaput!

But when I read a second ECK book, *The Spiritual Notebook*, also by Paul Twitchell, it shook me up badly.

In chapter 5, "The Creative Techniques," Paul introduces what he calls the Spiritual Exercises of ECK. He taught methods to turn the spiritual words I read about into real experience. One could go into the heavens while still alive in the physical body! Great! But there was a catch.

Would I Dare?

I had no problem *believing* that. My problem was would I dare *experience* it?

It's one thing for a young boy to ask a girl for a kiss, sure that she will say no and give him the escape clause in a contract he hadn't the know-how or guts to fulfill. But a problem arises for him if she says yes!

I was at such a crossroads.

I had sought truth, spiritual reality, everywhere. I had asked Truth for a kiss, and sure enough, she sprang forward and offered her lips via *The Spiritual Notebook*.

Paul had put down a simple formula. Do this, and Truth will stand before you in all her beauty. But instead of joy and enthusiasm, for me it was a time of trembling. I had got more than I had bargained for.

The possibility of getting out of the body was suddenly very real. But fear said, what if I became lost in some corner of heaven? I could see both my poor body and family waiting in vain for me to return. What a woeful day that would be!

And so I had sat trembling at the starting block, wishing I had not looked so deeply into Paul's book. I knew inside that if I refused to try these exercises, I would never rest again, ever. But to try them was terror.

Possibility of Getting Out of the Body

In those days, I had this notion that the first HU I sang would project me straight into some inner world without a moment's delay. Paul Twitchell made it sound so easy in his book. I never thought it was something one would have to work on persistently and with studied regularity.

So the two emotions—to try or not to try—fought a battle inside me for two months. Fear said, "Leave well enough alone." Curiosity said, "Proceed, or you'll never rest!"

In the end, by a small margin, the latter won.

I gritted my teeth and sang HU for a few minutes one evening. I had one eye on the inner world and the other out here.

Sometimes it pays to be a coward, I thought. If something in there threatened me, I could always jump back to safer ground out here in the familiar physical world.

Nothing happened.

Absolutely nothing happened.

I was both relieved and disappointed—and for the

same reason: relieved because nothing threatening happened, but at the same time disappointed because, well, something astounding should have happened! Paul Twitchell sounded too honest and straightforward to have sold me a bill of goods.

I Fixed Regular Times

This is when the former training I had undergone with the Catholic rosary came into use. If there was some secret to this HU thing, I had to discover it. I was going to sing HU until either one or both of us gave up!

I fixed regular times for the spiritual exercises— five o'clock in the morning and ten o'clock at night each day. I would sing HU unfailingly for at least twenty minutes each time. Ten o'clock was when the family had gone to bed and I had the family lounge all to myself. At five o'clock, no one was awake yet.

I continued with the HU routine twice a day because I could feel there was something substantial about the teachings of Eckankar.

Something Substantial

These teachings had passed a couple of tests from me. First, I found no hidden agendas in the teachings, where somebody was trying to take advantage of the public. Nor were there any no-go areas; no question was considered awkward—we could question everything.

Second, I received no threats or ultimatums about what would happen if I rejected the teachings. Life was an open, endless learning process, and each one of us came to each stage of the race in our own good time. The only competitor anyone had was oneself.

One evening, before I even started singing HU, I received a surprise.

"Why don't you believe in the Mahanta?" asked a

voice that seemed to come from within me. This was on June 2, 1991, when I sat down for my usual evening contemplation at ten o'clock.

This question brought me face-to-face with another problem—besides my fear of doing the Spiritual Exercises of ECK—that I had with the teachings of Eckankar. It concerned the Mahanta, the Living ECK Master.

Questions about the Mahanta

I had enjoyed reading about the ECK teachings because they rang true. Yet, I had some hard questions about the Mahanta. Was someone selling Jesus through the back door, calling him the Mahanta? Would God delegate such enormous powers as the Mahanta is said to have to a mere human being, considering what our politicians and dictators do with the little power they have?

I had solved that problem by filtering the Mahanta out of my ECK practices altogether!

When I think about that now, I am amused. I did not know it then, but I was trying to prepare fruit salad without fruit in it!

But I was sincere; and the Mahanta's patience knows no bounds. Finally, he helped me out during that spiritual exercise.

Inner Answer

A list sprang up before my inner eyes during that spiritual exercise even before I started singing HU. I closed my physical eyes so I could see it more clearly.

The list had two columns. The left column described the mission of Jesus as a world savior, and the right column showed the mission of the Mahanta as the Wayshower.

Jesus takes the sins, or misdemeanors, of his adherents upon himself, regardless of whether or not they understand the import of their actions. All they need do for these burdens to be lifted is to say, "I believe."

The Mahanta, on the other hand, leads his followers to a practical understanding of shortcomings within themselves. He connects them to the Light and Sound of God and shows them how to get off the karmic wheel and attain spiritual freedom.

Jesus dies as the sacrificial lamb to save (i.e., provide a haven, or heaven, for those who believe). But the Mahanta redeems by helping individuals work off their karma and achieve self-mastery. He does this via the ECK initiation, and sometimes by serving as a holding tank, then passing karma into the ECK Life Stream or regulating it for his chelas (disciples, or spiritual students of ECK).

The body imbued with a million fireflies, which I had encountered in my Lagos-weekend experience, now made sense. I now understood the sudden hunger for God that I had developed after that experience.

As I scanned this list, it became obvious: The missions of the Mahanta and Jesus ran on parallel lines that would never ever meet, much less clash.

Direct Experience

In all my life, I had never met a teacher who came during prayers to speak to me this directly.

"OK," I heard myself say inwardly, "I buy this program of yours, Mahanta!"

More surprises were in store for me that evening.

Unbelievably good tingly warmth surrounded my body on the yellow couch that evening, causing me goose pimples all over.

When I sang HU that night, I began to penetrate

into the inner worlds or heavens. I began to find answers to old questions about life as never before.

Public-Opinion Polls

One of my early tests in Eckankar concerned contention with public opinion.

Political Office

About a year or two after I met the Living ECK Master in Lagos, I was elected chairman in local government. I was now someone in the public eye.

One of my mentors, a Catholic, felt he was grooming me for the state governorship. When he heard that I had left the Church for "God-knows-what," he came over and questioned me.

"You had a front pew in church!" he said. "So why this?" he asked, with a sweep of his hand.

There was no way to make this man understand that spirituality, for me, went beyond having a front pew in church. The teachings of ECK were something I had searched for this whole lifetime—and apparently, many lifetimes before. But there was no way I could explain it to this fellow without offending him. I therefore kept silent.

"How Many Members?"

"How many members does Eckankar have in this state?" he went on. Then he paused in what had been more or less a soliloquy up to now.

"Less than fifty in this state," I answered, exaggerating. We were not just less than fifty; we were far less—perhaps less than half that.

He left his next question hanging:

And you are going to risk losing millions of Christian votes for this stupidity?

His reasoning was perfect—for someone else!

A Catholic priest had won the state governorship, presumably on the Christian vote, at the time I had won the chairmanship. His opponent was also a Christian, but the clever opposition had demonized him as a Muslim convert because of his supposed association with the spiritual head of Islam in Nigeria.

I refrained from telling my would-be mentor that I had no idea God was into politics. I wanted to keep our friendship—what remained of it.

It had not been much of a conversation. But it was a notable side effect of my matriculation into ECK.

Wrong Prayer

At one stage of Its journey, Soul looks to God for favors. But after being in ECK for a while, I began to realize that the supreme mission of Soul is to do something for God, not ask for favors.

When Soul is seeking God to receive favors, It has a tendency to use wrong prayer. In my early days in Eckankar, I tried this self-serving ploy. The lesson I got from my attempt was indelible.

Useful Spiritual Exercise

In *The Living Word*, Book 1, Sri Harold Klemp, the spiritual leader of Eckankar, outlines a useful exercise.

If one is about to travel, and the negative forces have come together to frustrate one's journey, then one can do a special spiritual exercise. He visualizes himself at the place where the journey starts and also at where the journey ends. Next he visualizes sweeping a path to clear the way to his destination. Then, like the lord of his own universe, he inwardly commands the driver or pilot (as the case may be) to proceed.

This visualization technique comes with a warning: Never substitute it for bad planning! One must first have a valid contract with the carrier (road, air, or water) before trying this exercise and use the technique only to clear up intrusive resistance from the negative forces.[2]

A Lesson in the Making

As chairman for my local government, I traveled to Lagos to solicit help from the Federal Environmental Protection Agency. In those days, local governments were poorly funded. To avoid the high hotel bills, I had planned not to sleep over in Lagos. I therefore told my official driver to pick me up at the Abuja airport in the evening.

"Even if the last flight from Lagos is announced and you don't see me, be assured that I will return," I told the driver. I told him to go to the Agura Hotel in Abuja in that case and to wait for me in the parking lot.

Go Slow

On the day of my visit to Lagos, it rained. Now Lagos, due to clogged drains, had flooded streets. This caused terrible traffic jams known as "go slow" in Nigeria. And it was particularly terrible that day. It looked as if I was going to miss the last flight back to Abuja, and the prospect of staying in Lagos was not rosy at all.

With more experience under my belt now, I would never do what I did. But when I was stuck in traffic around Tafawa Balewa Square and the sun had dipped over the horizon, I turned my attention to the above-mentioned visualization technique. I visualized myself stuck in the traffic jam at Tafawa Balewa Square; then I saw myself back in Abuja. I drew a powerful line with light between the two points and swept away all obstacles, mentally seeing myself arrive safely and on time in Abuja.

The fact that I had not got to the airport, much less bought a ticket, and therefore had no valid contract with any airline, was of little consequence to me then. All I thought about was not having to spend the night in Lagos.

The taxi driver, knowing my predicament, fought the Lagos gridlock, changing lanes and ducking into side streets to help me catch my flight. We finally got to the domestic wing of the Murtala Mohammed International Airport in one piece, thank God.

I snatched my bag and waved good-bye to the taxi driver. However, when I got to the ticket counter, I was informed that the last Nigeria Airways flight had already left for Abuja.

First Surprise

Disappointed, I took my bag and walked out of the terminal. I found the first surprise awaiting me.

Anyone who is familiar with Lagos taxi drivers knows that they try to pack twenty-five hours into one day and sometimes they appear to succeed. Our contract had ended when he dropped me off, so the taxi driver should have shot off like a bat out of hell to get the most out of the day before darkness fell. But he was sitting in his vehicle, waiting with the engine running to make sure I got a flight to Abuja. When I shook my head, he said, "Jump in! We'll go to Okada."

Okada Air was actually a local airline in Nigeria. *Okada* has since become a generic term for local, privately operated transportation. Even motorcycles for hire have adopted the term.

When the taxi driver took me to Okada Air, he followed me in and made sure there was a flight for me.

He refused extra payment.

When I pulled out money to pay for my ticket to Abuja, the ground crew told me to walk to the tarmac. "The plane is already out there," they said. "They will collect your money at the door."

We Were All Waiting for You!

As soon as I paid and boarded the plane, the air hostess closed the door.

A neighbor from home was already seated in the plane. Since the seat beside him was empty, I sat next to him.

"It appears we were all waiting for you!" he said. An alarm sounded in my head.

"What do you mean?" I asked, looking for a hint of leg-pulling from him. He appeared serious.

"This flight has been delayed for over one hour," he said. "No one told us why."

The alarm sounded even louder in my head.

Had I delayed this flight?

What were the consequences?

In the plane, my neighbor suggested we drive through the night to get home and thus avoid any hotel bills in Abuja. That suited me fine. I assured him that my driver would be waiting to take us on the three-hour journey.

When we arrived in Abuja, I raised my eyes to the wall clock at the Nnamdi Azikiwe International Airport. The time was exactly eight o'clock. I scanned the faces of the waiting crowd for my driver.

Consequences

He was not there.

"When they announced the last Nigeria Airways flight," I said, "my driver must have left." But I told him

I had foreseen such a circumstance. "He will be at the Agura," I assured him, "because that is where he was to wait for me."

But unbeknown to me, it was going to be a unique night and a poignant spiritual lesson.

We took a taxi to the Agura Hotel. A thorough search of the parking lot yielded nothing.

"Drivers are like that," said a second man, who had joined us. He was attending a seminar, and he gave us a lift to check both for the driver and a hotel room for the night. My two companions went into a long discourse about the bad behavior of government drivers. I did not agree with their assessment of the situation, for two reasons.

For one, my driver was an excellent and dependable fellow. He had driven me for a long time, even before I became chairman. Secondly, I *knew* what was going on.

I Knew What Was Going On

This situation was the result of wrong prayer in Lagos. I knew I would have to wait patiently to see how the payment for this karma would pan out.

Without the car, going home tonight was out. I had to find a hotel room for the night. Yet, I kept returning to the Agura car lot, checking for the vehicle and its driver, till a half hour before midnight.

One reason for this persistence was that most hotels in Abuja were sold out that evening! With not even a car to sleep in, it appeared that all that was left for me was to become a "floor member"—that is, to sleep on the floor somewhere.

When all other attempts to get a hotel room had failed, we had no alternative but to approach absolutely the most expensive hotel in the country at the time, the Nicon Noga Hilton Hotel, as it was called in those days.

Finally, I found a room here—for a higher price than I would have paid in Lagos. But I was grateful. At least I would not have to sleep on the floor after all.

Next Day

Next day, before six o'clock in the morning, I went to the Agura Hotel.

My official car was not in the parking lot.

After visiting the place intermittently till about nine o'clock without spotting the vehicle, I told my companions to go home without me. I would remain to search for my driver.

I then hired a taxi that shuttled me between the airport and Agura Hotel five or six times between nine in the morning and six in the evening.

At the airport, I combed the arrival lounge for the driver. Then I went out to the parking lot.

Abuja did not yet have such a high population then, so the parking lot did not have many vehicles in it. I searched the parking lot to no avail. Both driver and vehicle seemed to have dissolved into thin air!

As the taxi driver drove me back to town, I arranged with him to check with me at seven o'clock the next morning. We had agreed upon a fare for him to drive me back home if I did not find the driver and the car.

I had checked out of the Hilton that morning before I went in search of the car and driver. It was now Friday evening. The seminars in Abuja that had caused all reasonably priced hotels to be sold out seemed to be over. Today, I found a room in the less pricey Agura.

HU Song

I knew that the ECK center at home held a Friday HU Song at six-thirty in the evening. I decided to join in from my hotel room in Abuja.

Because I was so tired, I fell asleep during the thirty-minute HU song.

The ringing of my bedside telephone woke me up. When I put the receiver to my ear, my driver's voice came on the line.

I looked at the clock on the bedside table. It was exactly eight o'clock—twenty-four hours since I had returned from Lagos.

"What happened?" I asked my driver when he came up to my room.

Karmic Payback

He had waited for me the previous day till the last Nigeria Airways flight had been announced. Since I wasn't on it, he decided to carry out the instructions I had given him. But halfway back to town, both headlights of my official vehicle cut out! He drove the last fifteen minutes into Abuja with only streetlights to light the way.

Since he knew I might want to drive through the night to save on hotel bills, he decided to go and find a car-parts dealer to buy replacement headlights. After a long search, he found a parts dealer. Then he had to search for an electrician and get the lights fixed. He then returned to the Agura Hotel.

Then this morning, before six o'clock, he dashed to the airport in case I arrived on the first flight from Lagos. According to him, he had been sitting in the arrival lounge at the airport all day till the last flight was announced and I was apparently not on it. So he decided to return to the Agura. At the reception desk, he was assured that I was checked in, and they used the house phone to dial my room.

I Understood

After a while, I understood what might have happened.

While I searched for my driver and car, the ECK must have placed a shield between us. This was one reason we couldn't see each other.

By misusing the visualization technique, I had delayed an airplane full of people for one hour. I considered my twenty-four hour delay to be quite reasonable payback, since the plane had held more than twenty-four people.

Interestingly, what I was trying to avoid in Lagos—the high hotel bills—not only became my lot but almost doubled here in Abuja. The extra payment for the one-day taxi hire was thrown in for good measure.

The best prayer, I have found out, is to sing HU and let God do the rest—sometimes even when I do have a valid contract and things are not going the way they should. It's safer!

The Downside of Gossip

At the beginning stages of my study of dreams, the Master brought me face-to-face with the fact that gossip is a spiritual dead end. Where their paths cross, people can become privy to other people's lives. And the student of the Mahanta learns to respect others' privacy.

Soapsuds

In the dream state, I set out to visit a friend I will call Prince, who lived with his girlfriend. I knocked at the door, and since it was not locked, I walked in. I thought nobody was there at first. Then Prince's girlfriend emerged from the bathroom, wearing nothing but soapsuds! Her eyes were tightly closed against the stinging soapsuds.

I withdrew quickly and discreetly before she could open her eyes and discover me, to our mutual embarrassment.

A Test

Prince and I were both ECKists. Our discussions often centered on our inner experiences to support each other's spiritual adventures in Eckankar. Therefore, when I met him later, what I thought to be a snippet of rare humor from the inner worlds was too much not to share.

As it turned out, this dream was a test from the Mahanta. But how was I to know?

Prince convulsed with laughter as he listened to me tell about my dream. When he brought his guffaws under control, he would ask me for a few details to check on whether I'd really had a ringside seat.

Not Amused

Later, to my horror, Prince told me he had told his girlfriend about my dream experience, thinking that, like him, she would see the funny side to it. To spice up his story, he threw in a few details I had never spoken about but which he was privy to. And then he was surprised that his girlfriend was not amused!

From then on, the girl started acting very cold toward me. When she could, she began to avoid me completely. She thought I was using my ability at Soul Travel to spy on her!

I had never been so embarrassed in my life.

But that was not the end of the story.

Inner Satsang

Four days later, I had a dream where the Mahanta, the Living ECK Master came to teach an ECK Satsang (spiritual instruction) class in our area. The welcoming committee had given me the responsibility of booking an appropriate hotel where the Mahanta would stay the night.

As I sat in his class, my mind was so taken up with my responsibility that I hardly heard what he was talking about. But suddenly I heard the words: "I don't like people who hurt others with their unfeeling attitude."

For some reason I couldn't put my finger on, those words bothered me.

When the Satsang class was over, we lined up to greet the Master.

"Can I hug you?" I asked the Mahanta.

"Yes," Sri Harold said, after some hesitation, "you may hug me."

But before I could do that, someone who had not asked permission rushed in and hugged the Master ahead of me.

Two Strange Things

When my turn came to hug the Master, Sri Harold took off his shirt and put a pure white, thick terry towel around his shoulders. When I approached, two strange things occurred.

First, the Master turned his back to me.

Secondly, he seemed to have grown extremely tall. I stretched up my arms to hug him, but they barely reached his waist. So I just pressed them to his sides—not a very satisfactory hug—and got out of line.

When I woke up, there was no question in my mind about the "unfeeling attitude" referred to in the dream.

It was about the events of four days earlier. I had been given an inner experience, which had been a test. It mattered little that the person I revealed the experience to was the dream subject's boyfriend. My sharing the experience had hurt someone.

Purity

When the Master took his shirt off and covered his torso with the white terry towel, he was telling me that what the ECK exposes to us in a dream is to be treated with respect and purity of heart—not gossiped about or treated as something trifling or made the subject of a joke. By treating it so lightly, I had become a spiritual midget, and the Master's face was turned away from me because of that action.

What I had thought of as such a hilarious joke was not so funny anymore.

Law of Silence

This was one of the most embarrassing incidents I experienced since taking up the dream teachings of ECK. Perhaps it was the only way the lesson could have hit home.

After this, I began to consciously restrain my urge to discuss my inner experiences. One easy and safe way I found to deal with this was to write such experiences in monthly initiate reports to the Master. As I did that on a regular basis, I began to get a handle on the Law of Silence.

Leaving the Church

As I mentioned earlier, the hunger I developed for God after a dream encounter with the Mahanta

("Mr. Fireflies") during a weekend in Lagos led me into the Catholic Church.

I had found great joy and company among the Catholics. However, once I found Eckankar and realized its teachings suited me better, I decided it would be more honest to leave the Church. But in the dream state, the Mahanta warned me that it was not yet time to leave.

I had unfinished business—if not with the Catholic Church as a whole, at least with this parish and the parish priest.

Through the Back Door

In this dream, I find myself dragging a large iron box, returning to the church—through the back door.

When I get in, I am a bit embarrassed to find myself in the bedroom of the parish priest. He is not at all embarrassed. As a matter of fact, he is overjoyed to see me.

Even though I consider the room warm, the parish priest not only has a lively fire roaring in the fireplace, he has also covered himself in a thick, white blanket. The parish priest's hair is a mane of pure white wool.

Contemplating on this dream, I understood that the iron box represented the old karmic ties I had with the Church and this priest. The back-door entrance was an indication that I would no longer occupy a front pew in this church. I was only here to pay an old debt.

The fire he had made and the thick blanket the priest covered himself in were indications that even though the spiritual climate of this church was fine for others—certainly the parish priest—it was a teaching that was presently out of season for me.

The white hair the priest had in the dream was a humorous anecdote.

On the outer (in the physical world), the priest had

dark hair. But some time after this dream, I learned that the priest had been dyeing his hair on a regular basis. Apparently, he forgot to dye the hair on his astral body, so that transfiguration stopped with his physical body!

Live Cow in Church

During the Harvest and Bazaar Thanksgiving that year, the parish priest called on me to discuss what gift I intended to give to the Church. When I told him, he suggested that, for just a little more expense, I could offer a live cow to the Church.

It was a shrewd move indeed, as things turned out.

In Tivland (part of Nigeria), in 1927, the British colonial government banned the traditional exchange marriage. A dowry system was introduced to replace the exchange of women between families. At first, the cow, the largest domestic animal known to the Tiv, took the place of the woman who was lost to another family in marriage. The cow could later be exchanged for a wife to replace a "lost" daughter or sister.

The prestige of the cow thus rose above its status as an animal. It now represented a human being, and many important rituals were built around the cow. To offer a cow for anything is to accord that thing the greatest place of honor.

The parish priest was quite aware of this important symbolism in the socio-religious and cultural life of the people. I did not know it at the time, but the priest had plans to use my family's cow gift to boost his church activities.

On the day of the Harvest and Thanksgiving Mass, the parish priest insisted I lead the cow into church, followed by members of my family, and proceed right up to the altar.

When we arrived at the altar with the cow, the priest dipped his broom deeply into the bucket of holy water, then sent a gust of spray in our direction that an ocean wave crashing on the beach could have envied. The congregation screamed in delight like a crowd of teenagers seeing their favorite pop star onstage.

Come the next Thanksgiving, no fewer than five families brought live cows into church for the holy-water ceremony! The momentum of giving picked up and became a tremendous fund-raising boost for the church. The priest soon completed a new and much larger congregational hall—a project that had started four years earlier but stalled.

But it mystified both the priest and laity that when the congregation moved into the new church building, I did not follow. I stayed home on Sundays, since there were no ECK Worship Services in those days in our area.

Time to Leave

The Mahanta let me know very clearly in a dream that it was now time to leave. I had paid my dues to the priest and, hopefully, the Catholic Church.

In the dream state, I've been traveling, and I return just before daybreak to the new church building. It looks as if a hurricane has hit and all but destroyed the new building. The roof has been blown off, and doors and windows hung askew on their hinges.

Surely, no one lives here anymore, *I think. But to my surprise, as I approach the entrance, someone opens the door from inside. It is the parish priest.*

"I have two boxes in the rafters," I tell the parish priest upon entering. "Please bring down the wooden box. As to the iron box, I have no more use for it."

However, when the priest gets up into the rafters, he

instead drops the iron box down to me.

"Never mind," I say and go up into the rafters for the wooden box, which I plan to leave with.

Then I woke up in my bed. As I thought about the dream, its meaning became clear.

The destroyed church signified that the Church's teachings had lost their relevance in my present spiritual life. In other words, I needed to move out of that classroom into another that would better meet my spiritual needs.

The wooden box symbolized the timeless teachings of the church that are not in conflict with the living Shariyat, the action and influence of Divine Spirit in our daily life. Such teachings are embodied in statements like Love your neighbor as yourself. But the priest still wanted to present the traditional and social doctrines of the Church—the iron box that I had no use for anymore. His action in the dream state would spill over into the physical, showing up as a refusal to let me go.

Dodo Come Back to Life

This was all during the time of my local-government chairmanship, and the era of the cell phone was not yet upon us. The telephone in my office worked fine, but the one at home, in the official residence, refused to oblige. Repeated complaints to the authorities and constant repairs never yielded any positive result for more than a couple of days. After a while, it got to where I never bothered to complain to the authorities anymore; I just let sleeping phones lie. So, even though I was the chief security officer of the local government, I had no phone contact with the world after I closed my office for the day.

I was therefore surprised when I returned from a meeting in the state capital one evening. My wife informed me that our (former) parish priest had called and wanted me to return his call.

"On which phone?" I asked.

She pointed to our phone that had declared a perpetual strike the whole time we had lived there. As I lifted the handset to my head, I could hardly believe my ear.

The dial tone made me feel as if I were witnessing a dodo come back to life in our living room. I dialed the number, and the reverend father answered as promptly as if he had been waiting by the phone.

"Could you and your wife come over this evening?" he asked breezily.

Still a Friend

Even though I had stopped going to church when the congregation moved into the new church building, my wife and I still considered the parish priest a friend. We often sat with him over drinks and snacks, passing a pleasant evening in his parish residence. The tone of his telephone invitation made me believe this was going to be one of those evenings.

I was wrong.

My wife and I swept into the front yard of the parish priest's residence. Not a single vehicle was in evidence. Everything spoke of a quiet evening.

Like a ground spider that had felt the web to its lair shaken by a potential victim, the parish priest materialized on the veranda, oozing the friendly demeanor of the excellent host he always had been.

His residence was in the back. And that is where he had always welcomed us. But today, he came to welcome us in the front yard. And if I had been alert, I should have wondered why.

When he led us into the main lounge of the parish residence, we reeled in shock.

Who's Who of the Parish

A meeting of the who's who of the parish was in progress. They were making plans for the next Thanksgiving bazaar. Apparently, so as not to alarm us and precipitate a hasty retreat, the parish priest had advised his distinguished visitors to park out of sight on the inner courtyard. He must have further advised them to keep both their voices and profiles low when our car arrived, making the place appear quiet in spite of the large crowd inside.

As we recovered from our shock, I observed the great satisfaction on the face of the priest for having pulled off this caper.

Why Have You Not Moved with Us?

We were shown to our seats at the table. We had hardly settled in, when the chairman of the bazaar committee, a lawyer, bore into me as if I was a witness in court.

"Your contributions to the new church building were as good as anybody's," he said, "so why have you not moved with us to the new building?"

At first, only anger seethed through my being. I was upset with the parish priest for pulling this kind of trick on us. This was an invasion of our psychic space for sure. The arrangement was to half intimidate us back into the fold.

Fortunately, I was not too mad to forget the HU. As I sang HU inwardly, calmness began to wash over me.

Well-Meaning People

For one thing, I began to see that these were well-meaning people. A group member they considered important—an opinion molder—was about to bolt. Did

Christ not say that a good shepherd would leave ninety-nine sheep and go into the wilderness to look for the one that was lost?

And at the time, come to think of it, I was not just any sheep. I was a prize ram with a first-citizen tag in the influential local government. And Catholics thrive on social acceptance. It has always been a powerful tool for their longevity.

My anger subsided, because I could now see things from their point of view, even if I did not agree entirely with them or their methods. I began to calm down.

When the priest first took over, this had been a weak, out-of-the-way parish. He had managed to build it into a booming center of religious activities, which eventually attracted many people of influence. My offering of a cow for Thanksgiving had not been forgotten, as it was one of the actions that had upped the ante on other parishes' fund-raisers. Why should this priest allow his prize ram to take a walk without some effort to return him to the fold?

Things now appeared in stark clarity: his aim was to keep me; mine was to escape—and hurt as few feelings as possible in the process.

Graceful Way

There must be a graceful way out of all this, I thought, recalling that the Mahanta had declared 1992–93 A Year of Graceful Living. And so I asked the Mahanta inwardly to help me find that graceful balance so that I could be free to leave without offending the sensibilities of a well-meaning group.

The solution was a surprise even to me. I can never fully recapture what happened that night.

The chairman repeated his question and asked when they should expect me back. He and the members of his committee sat waiting for an answer.

The words came to me as I began to speak.

Journey of Many Seasons

"I am on a journey of many seasons," I recall saying.

"Such a journey takes one over high mountains and through deep valleys. And if one walks in a straight line long enough, one is bound to return to the same spot in the end, since the world is round."

Heads around the table nodded like agama lizards, silently agreeing even though they couldn't guess where it was all going. Neither could I, at first!

"But could anyone, after undertaking such a journey, still remain the same?"

Heads shook silently, like horses shaking dew from their manes.

"I must complete that journey. I believe the scriptures say, 'As it was in the beginning, is now, and ever shall be, world without end.'"

And every throat around the table chorused, "Amen!"

Everybody, to my surprise, burst out into cheers and heartfelt applause. But I could see that this ambiguous answer did not set well with the legal-minded chairman. I have never known a lawyer that is a friend to ambiguity, except when it serves his purpose in court. Moreover, small groups around the table went into whispered arguments. They had apparently enjoyed the sound of the talk without knowing where it led them or was leading me—namely, in opposite directions! Now, in small groups, they were trying to decipher what my short speech meant.

Some whispered that I was coming back right away. Others said they understood that it might take time. And yet others wondered if I was coming back at all.

A Good-bye with Grace

I knew the lawyer would soon clear his throat and ask me to be a little bit more specific. I was wondering how I would be able to handle that, when the Mahanta broke into my thoughts inwardly.

"You have said your good-bye gracefully," he said. "Perhaps you should also leave gracefully while you can."

I took my wife's hand and got up. "I wish you the most fruitful deliberations," I said, flashing my best smile.

To my surprise, nobody tried to stop us with questions, talk, or even an offer of food or drink. They were too busy with the postmortem of the speech to bother with any of that. At that fortuitous juncture, we exited.

When we got back home, I picked up the phone to call the parish priest. I wanted to soften the abruptness of my exit. After all, he had tried his best, even if his action had seemed offensive to me at first.

My eyebrows shot up in surprise. True to its pedigree, the phone had once more gone into hibernation. There was no dial tone. It was dead as a dodo.

I thanked the Mahanta for helping me make this graceful good-bye to centuries-old friends and a great organization. Soon I would have new friends in the ECK community to fill the vacuum left by my voluntary excommunication.

The Last Drink

Even before I got into Eckankar, I was never a heavy imbiber of alcoholic drinks. I'd drink beer now and then with friends in the evening or at social occasions. But even early on in Eckankar, I recognized the importance of what I was getting from my dreams. I also knew that even the little alcohol I drank constituted an impediment to my total recall of these dreams.

One evening, I asked the Inner Master to help me stop drinking alcohol.

Born Again?

I recalled a friend of mine, back in our university days, who had become "born again." Through willpower and the persuasion of those who converted him, he had stopped drinking beer—for a while. But one hot day, while sitting with friends who were far from being "born again," he stumbled.

The heat and the sweating bottle of beer from the fridge that they placed before him were too much persuasion. He drank eight of them—perhaps to make up for lost time.

When he returned to campus, more than a little unsteady on his feet, the first person he met was Brother Basil, who had converted him and had the responsibility to see that he not backslide.

"Brother Douglas," Brother Basil called out breezily. But Brother Douglas was in no condition to be with the brotherhood at that moment. The old ways, alas, proved unconquerable. Being "born again" had been an academic exercise, and it had failed. Something inside him craved the old life, and his conversion had left that craving untouched.

I didn't have any intention of becoming another Brother Douglas.

Dagon and the Ark of the Covenant

If the ECK teachings are all they are cracked up to be, they will naturally get me to leave what I know is not good for me, I said to myself.

So I still housed Dagon and the Ark of the Covenant together in the same room—I still drank the odd beer and went on singing the HU. Not at the same time, of course! In a month's time, the HU began to show its power.

Hangover

On a particular outing, I drank just one beer. When I woke up the next day, I felt like someone who had drowned in a brewery vat! I couldn't believe it.

I was chairman of local government. But I had to miss work, thanks to *one* beer.

Something inside told me that beer was now poison to me. However, part of my mind said it was only beer in green bottles that caused this reaction.

I had heard that stouts—black stouts—are healthy and even medicinal. An ad for one popular brand had been "Guinness is good for you!" So I turned to stouts.

For two weeks, black stout was OK. After the two weeks, stout was still good—but only for someone else!

Another hangover of immense proportions hit me, keeping me from work for another day. And so my romance with black stout ended.

But I did not convert easily. I planned to avoid the trap Brother Douglas had fallen into.

Turn to wine—the civilized drink, part of my mind said. And so I began drinking wine only.

Last Alcoholic Drink

I drank wine, but I also set up a special sober time to sing the HU.

HU and wine cohabitated harmoniously—for a while. But one day, Dagon finally fell on its face and broke a leg and neck.

It happened when I hosted the state governor on his tour of the local government. At the end of his tour, I gave him and his large entourage a state luncheon. During this meal, I took three glasses of wine. They turned out to be my last use of alcoholic drink.

Afterward I returned to the chairman's official residence to rest. The wine seemed to have no effect on me till late evening.

I lay in bed to sleep. But sleep would not come even though I was tired. In fact, in all my life, before or since, I have never experienced such tiredness. I couldn't move a muscle. Yet, my brain was strangely lucid and on fire. I begged for the amnesia of sleep, but it would not come.

I felt like a lightbulb designed for sixty watts but compelled to carry a thousand! I became very scared. No sleep, no movement. What was I to do?

As I lay deathly still, it felt as if someone was going over my insides with a terrazzo grinding machine and industrial scouring brushes all at once. My ears rang as if with the roar of a lion. Then an impression like a waterfall began to send a powerful message through me. "You're finished with alcohol today! You're finished with alcohol today!" it said.

When the scouring brushes and the terrazzo grinding machine finally came gradually to a halt, I fell mercifully into a dreamless sleep.

True Inner Healing

Next morning, I woke up with no hangover, strangely enough. But the very thought of any alcoholic drink brought an immediate feeling of nausea.

It's been thirteen years as of this time of writing. I have never had the slightest desire for even a sip of any alcoholic drink—no matter how civilized.

No willpower was involved here. The Mahanta had given me one thing Brother Basil could never have given Brother Douglas—true inner healing!

Try this spiritual exercise today!

The Easy Way

Just before going to bed at night concentrate your attention on the Spiritual Eye, that place between the eyebrows. Chant HU or God inwardly or silently.

Hold your attention on a black screen in the inner vision, and keep it free of any pictures if at all possible. If you need a substitute for mental pictures flashing up unwantedly, put the image of the Living ECK Master in place of them.

After a few minutes of this, you may hear a faint clicking sound in one ear or the sound of a cork popping. You will suddenly find yourself outside the physical body, looking back at it in the room. Now you are ready for a short journey in the other worlds.

There is nothing to fear, for no harm can come to you while outside the body. Although you may not know it, the Mahanta will be standing by to keep watch over your progress. After a while the Soul body will return and slide gently into the physical self with hardly more than a very light jolt.

If this is not successful the first time, try it again, for the technique works. It has worked for others.

—Sri Harold Klemp
The Spiritual Exercises of ECK[3]

4
Pink Road to Heaven

The Second Plane is the Astral, or the emotional, world. It is the highest plane reached by astral projection and is the source of most occult sciences, ghosts, flying saucers, spirits, etc. The sound is that of the roaring sea. Its word, or chant, is Kala. *The ruler is Jot Niranjan.*

—*The Shariyat-Ki-Sugmad*, Books One & Two[1]

I met Dana on a trip to a seminar for local-government chairmen that took place a long way from home. It was a chance meeting—or so I thought.

I was two decades older than her. But shortly after we met, we were talking easily to each other and telling each other things normally shared between old, trusted friends.

The Rooster and the Hen

A secret alarm sounded inside me. Dana was single, but I was married and had a family. Yet, the interest Dana roused in me was more than cursory. Worse still, we lived in the same small town. It would be nigh impossible to hide an affair.

If my marriage had been troubled, I would have understood. But this was not the case at all. In fact my marriage was strong and, so far, secure. I had no reason whatever to be interested in someone this strongly. But what I felt could not be extinguished by logic. Why was I being so helplessly drawn into a situation that was bound to bring only trouble?

When I left the seminar, Dana gave me her address. Against my better judgment, I took it.

Back home, I wrestled with the compulsion to visit Dana. Within a week, I lost.

One day, as if the car I drove had a homing device guiding it to Dana's place, I ended up there.

I had hoped, knowing that I was only deluding myself, that a second meeting would somehow expose this attraction as nothing but a fleeting infatuation. Instead, things got worse. I was being drawn into quicksand, and it was no use trying to run. My desire to be with Dana had overwhelmed me.

Paradoxically, I loved my family just the same.

Soft Shoulder

Back home, I turned to the Inner Master for help. "I need to get out of this while my peace and that of others involved is still intact!" I cried. My plea was answered in the dream state that night.

I am a front-seat passenger in a jeep driven by the Mahanta on a narrow dirt road. It is night.

Behind us, a vehicle with its headlights blazing drives close to our bumper. I get the idea that the other vehicle behind us wants to pass.

"Why don't we pull over for it?" I ask the Mahanta.

"We'll get stuck on the soft shoulder," he responds and keeps driving, with that vehicle closely following.

Later on, I would understand the symbology of this part of the dream in contemplation.

The front vehicle I sat in was my state of consciousness. The Master was my "driver," or guide. I had surrendered the wheel of my life to him.

The vehicle behind, driving uncomfortably close to our rear bumper, was Dana. To abandon the relationship (let her vehicle pass) at this stage would get me bogged down in some emotional morass. The Master apparently was using this relationship to firm up that "soft ·shoulder" within my emotional fabric.

The dream continued.

Suddenly, there is no jeep and no Master in sight. I find myself with Dana in an abandoned mine with clear blue water like a swimming pool. We sit in the water back-to-back. The warmth between us is unbelievable. Then in a twinkling of an eye, I find myself at Dana's residence, where she lives alone with her mother. I sit in the open compound, eyes on Dana, like a love-struck teen.

Then I woke up.

I thought the abandoned mine might be a symbol for the minefield of emotions that we had been through in the past and had got into again in the present. The clear water was the Holy Spirit, healing us of whatever was wrong between us.

Intense emotions were the driving force in this relationship. I would soon discover just how intense.

The Incredible Hulk

One day, I drove to Dana's place and found a black saloon car (sedan) parked in my usual parking space. I had to park on the opposite side of the road. I would soon find out the meaning of this waking dream.

Inside, Dana sat on a love seat with a fellow that

reminded me of the comic-book character the Incredible Hulk.

I knew him back in secondary-school days as a member of the school football team, where he played central defense. He had a wide, deep chest, and he often had to stoop to enter doors that we normal humans walked through upright.

The look on Dana's face clearly said three's a crowd.

It was not hard to decipher who was making it a crowd.

I Can Take A Hint

I can take a hint, I thought. I said a hasty good-bye and stumbled back out the door. Dana gave me a half-hearted escort to the car and did not bother to cross the road to where Hulk had forced me to park. She seemed in a hurry to get back inside. I don't think she wanted Hulk to get anxious.

I sat down hard in the car, dazed and feeling very foolish. Had I misjudged our feelings as being mutual? Had I played the fool and misread everything?

I was far from happy, though I tried to tell myself I was better off for having this attraction I couldn't handle snatched out of my hands.

It's often so with situations like this. I had prayed to the Master for deliverance from this potentially destructive relationship. I should have been happy when I got what I'd asked for—and so quickly and dramatically. Instead, all I felt was depression, not elation.

What happens after this? I wondered.

Go home and forget it all, you fool, the mind said.

It's Not Over Yet

Well, thanks, Mahanta, for ending it this way, I said inwardly, without really feeling thankful.

It's not over yet, something inside said.

Was that the Inner Master speaking, or was it simply my attachment to the situation speaking? I wondered.

I was too shell-shocked and dazed to decide which was which. I simply slunk back home and tried to forget everything. But the pain would not disappear.

Dream-State Clinic

In the dream state, the Master took me to a clinic.

"If we give him the treatment," the matron in charge tells the Master, "he might react. We don't want to be responsible for that."

"I will take responsibility for him," the Master says.

The lady takes a large syringe and begins to rub it lengthwise on my stomach.

"She's not going to plunge that into my solar plexus, is she?" I ask inwardly as I break into a sweat.

On the outer, I never took an injection I could dodge. I knew that rabies injections were usually administered through the navel. It had always been my prayer that I would never have to take such an injection. But here in this dream, even though I had not suffered a rabid dog bite (or was it a love bite?), I was about to be given just such an injection.

Gently, the lady inserts the needle into my navel.

I have averted my eyes, afraid to watch. But in my peripheral vision I see that she has drawn red fluid, like blood, into the syringe. Now she inserts the needle just under my left breast and empties the fluid into my heart.

I called this dream Solar-Plexus-to-Heart Healing. Symbolically, I thought the Master was transferring emotional "gut" feelings to the heart. In other words, the Master was transferring my raw emotions for Dana to real love.

How this was going to pan out, I had no idea.

"Let's go home," the Master says.

I woke up in my bed.

Geography of the Past

When I awoke, the terrible emptiness that I had felt in my heart had all but gone. I would survive.

A few days later, the Master showed me, in the dream state, why this relationship had dropped such an emotional bomb on me.

I find myself at the site office of a big building project. The Master is in charge here. As he continues with his work, he gives me several atlases to peruse. These atlases are actually the "geography" of my past relationships with Dana.

I apologize to the Master for taking so much of his time. He waves that aside. "Be my guest!" he says breezily.

I realized later that my presence here with him for so long was part of the healing process.

When I have perused all the material given to me, I excuse myself and go outside. In the open yard stands the hulking steel structure under construction. It is several stories high.

To me, the iron structure symbolized the Kal—the works of the negative power.

"Why did Hermann commit suicide?" the Master asks me telepathically.

In an instant, I slip into the mindset of someone contemplating suicide.

There are no tomorrows or even yesterdays. Life is blank, without joy or even sadness. It is just something to be gotten rid of—like rubbish or stale rheum.

I walk like an automaton toward the high-rise steel

structure and ascend to the top. From the top, I throw myself down, belly-first.

As I fall to certain death, no emotions stir as the air rushes past me. To a bystander, I might even look bored.

Very Much Alive

My body hits the ground with a whump and breaks apart. But that's as far as my attempt to extinguish my life goes. I feel no pain as I immediately leave the body.

I get up from the ground in my Astral body, very much alive. The life I have tried to send into oblivion is still very much around. I stand up confused, wondering what to do next. I was looking for oblivion—not this!

The Master climbs down to this marshy area where I stand. As he approaches, I notice two youths nearby.

And what followed in the dream indicated that I had committed suicide for the same reason in two other lifetimes.

Smoke in the Master's Face

As the Master approaches, one youth pulls on a cigarette then blows smoke in the Master's face! The second youth repeats the scandalous act.

Smoking in the presence of the Master is like blasphemy—just like suicide!

I realize (even as I dream) that the youths' actions symbolize my second and third suicides. I have now "blown smoke in the Master's face" three times like this!

The Master wrinkles his nose each time and moves on toward me.

"Don't these youth know that one is not allowed to smoke in the presence of the Mahanta?" I ask inwardly. I am now speaking from my present state of consciousness, where I have at last realized that one should not "smoke in

the presence of the Master"—that suicide is a spiritual crime against Soul, a vain attempt to cheat or defy God.

The Master fixes his eyes on me for a minute or so.

"Come, come and listen to the rooster and the hen!" the Master whispers telepathically.

I begin to listen. I listen intently for a while and even hold my breath to catch the faintest of sounds. But listening as hard as I can, all I hear are the croaking frogs in this marshy area. I cannot hear any hens or roosters.

Then I woke up in bed.

Recording Dreams Immediately

I had the habit of recording dreams immediately when I wake up. That way, I often catch important details that I would otherwise miss if I left it for too long. Because of that, I always keep pen and paper at my bedside.

But when I tried to put pen to paper this time, a powerful nudge told me to go and record this dream in my study.

Even though the study was some way away, I obeyed the nudge and went there. That room had a large window facing the street. In minutes, I was glad I obeyed the nudge.

Two Roosters and One Hen

When I recorded the Master's last words—*Come, come and listen to the rooster and the hen*—I began to hear the sound of chickens outside! I put down my pen, rushed to the window, and drew the curtains.

A large number of hens and a few roosters had rushed into the empty lot on the other side of the street. As I watched with curiosity, the main body of fowls peeled off into the undergrowth, leaving two roosters and one hen as if on a stage.

One rooster was massive. He made me think of the

Incredible Hulk at Dana's place about a week earlier. The other, a midget in comparison, was closer to my proportions. Both male birds had an interest in the hen.

The bigger rooster scratched in the dirt, apparently found a tasty morsel there, and called to the hen. She bounded up to him and stayed close as the massive rooster fed her the tasty morsel.

By his body language, I could tell the midget rooster's desire for the hen was all-consuming. But as far as the two lovers were concerned, he did not exist!

The midget seemed to be considering his chances. It must have looked suicidal to challenge that big rooster for that female.

I have never witnessed such distilled grief as I witnessed from a bird that morning. The midget rooster considered his chances and saw the possibility of winning that female drop to zero. He staggered from the site in a state which made me think that, had there been such a thing as suicide in roosterland, that midget would have headed for a six-story steel structure to end it all!

I sat down and pondered.

The reason for my attachment to Dana and my deep grief at losing her like this became apparent to me. In the past, I couldn't take the loss gracefully, so I had committed suicide—and then done two encores!

Now I became curious. What karmic debt caused Dana to abandon me, resulting in all this pain then and now?

Why Have You Kept Away from Me?

"Why have you kept away from me? We need to talk!" It was a note from Dana.

Kept away? I thought. *Had she not virtually shown me the gate?*

I wondered what to make of this message. But curiosity brought me once more to Dana. I drove up to her place expecting to see that black car parked in the parking lot. It was not there.

"Why have you kept away from me?" She repeated the question she had asked in her note.

I asked about Hulk.

"It's been over for a while."

That was quick, I said inwardly. But outwardly, I only looked at her, poker-faced. Dana interpreted my silence as disbelief, so she told me about her experience.

Hulk Had Three Wives

Hulk's sweet talk had won him three wives, whom he kept at home like trophies. At one time, there had been more. Dana discovered that he had intended to make her the fourth.

She realized that Hulk was mainly a conqueror. Once he got a woman into his harem, he lost interest and pursued more challenging customers. It was of little concern to him whether or not he left his old customers satisfied. Some left, while others stayed—like the three presently at home.

Dana had proved a challenge to him, and he had given it his all. He almost succeeded, till she caught on to his game.

There were some apologies between us. But I also realized that the Mahanta had introduced this other relationship to help me catch my wind. What was there to do now that that burning emotional fire was gone?

Karmic Connections

In place of the emotional fire, over time I began to feel protective instead of passionate toward Dana. But I was not quite sure in which direction to sail. Would it be *away from* or *along with* this person? So I asked the Mahanta whether it was time to leave.

The advice came in a dream.

As I stand in this place, a tall woman who looks like an African-American comes and grabs me from behind. She is much taller than I, so she asks me to get up on a higher platform and "kiss me properly." I know right away that this is Dana in a past incarnation.

"I like the way you treat me. Never abandon me like you did before!" she says with vehemence.

I woke up with more questions: Me? Abandoned her? When had I abandoned Dana?

Was that the reason she had also abandoned me in the past, causing me to commit suicide? And then recently abandoned me for Hulk in this life, causing me so much pain?

It was New Year's Day. The family went out without me. I needed some rest.

Alone in the house, I looked for some reading material. I happened to pick *Earth to God, Come In Please . . .* , a book about real-life experiences ECKists around the world have with the Mahanta.

I Burst into Tears

I was reading these stories casually, till I came upon the story of a young single mother who had given her daughter up for adoption. It was not that she did not love the girl, but because in her financial situation, she could not adequately support the child. I was reading how, at Christmastime, she knitted some clothes—putting all her love into the job—to send anonymously to the child she had had to give up.[2]

Suddenly and inexplicably, to my great surprise and embarrassment, I burst into tears!

I come from a society where men are not supposed to cry—certainly not over a single girl who gives up a child she loves because she has no economic wherewithal to support the child. But here I was, not just sniffling but crying my eyes out over what some men—and possibly myself in the past—would sniff at as a sissy story.

I couldn't believe this was happening to me!

The Mahanta Was Letting Me Heal

I was glad the family was away. How could I have explained these tears to them?

I sobbed and wept in turns. The story rocked me to the core.

The Mahanta was letting me heal from the past-life karma with Dana.

I discovered that in a past life when I had been with Dana out of wedlock, she had apparently reincarnated with me not for the material benefits I could give her, but just the love, which I had plenty of in my heart for her. By giving her up in that life, I had hurt her deeply and created a karmic debt. Therefore she chose lifetimes in which I was vulnerable and left me for another. It had hurt so badly that I committed suicide each lifetime it happened. In this life, the Mahanta had brought us together once again to balance things out— to help us deal with the love we had been looking for from each other without success.

Spiritual Lessons

In the dream state, Dana and I got married. "It's strictly separate bedrooms!" the Mahanta, who presided over the wedding, said in wry humor. This inner wedding was to help us complete the residual karma between us.

I now understood a Soul Travel experience I'd had earlier with Dana. In that experience we met not as human bodies but as two energy fields embracing each other. "We are to love each other in this life—without marriage!" I had heard myself telling her.

Dana eventually married someone else.

The Master showed me in a dream that, had we married, we would have lived in bliss but completely missed the spiritual lessons provided by our present spouses—lessons we are each in dire need of to take the next spiritual step in our lives.

Without the Master's help, who knows whether our karmic debts would have grown worse instead of better?

Try this spiritual exercise today!

Formula Two Technique

This technique helps us visit the Astral Plane, where we can find out why we have certain emotional connections with people around us.

First, record in your dream journal that you are using this technique.

Chant HU two times, then breathe two times. Keep doing this for fifteen minutes, before bed or in contemplation. Lightly keep in mind that you want to visit the Astral Plane, the plane of emotion.

Record your dreams next morning and note their significance.

—Adapted from "The Formula Technique"
in *The Spiritual Exercises of ECK*
by Harold Klemp[3]

5

Twisting the Tail of Destiny

The Mahanta is the distributor of karma in this world, and what he says is the word of the Sugmad. All the Lords of Karma are under his hand and must do as he directs. Hence, Eckankar is the spiritual refuge for all Souls.

—*The Shariyat-Ki-Sugmad*, Books One & Two[1]

———————————

Accuracy in the coincidence between affairs of the inner and outer worlds has provided great assurance about the teachings of ECK.

On the night of February 17–18, 2000, this dream came to me.

Third Initiation

After a long wait, the flight is called for boarding. I get up to wait in line.

I have been expecting a long line, since it appears our flight has been delayed. But I am surprised that, apart from me, only one person stands in line—an Asian-looking lady directly behind me.

I turn inquiring eyes on her. She responds with an inscrutable Mona Lisa smile. But she lets me know telepathically that she will be my companion for this flight.

Later, I would come to know her as Chung Soo Lee, a female ECK Master of Korean origin. The Master detailed her to watch over my welfare while I went through the heaven of memory.

Later, I am lined up to accept my graduation certificate from secondary school. Another line has formed close by for those graduates who are to move into a tertiary institution. I immediately join that line after I collect my graduation certificate from secondary school.

When I got my pink slip in the mail from the Mahanta—an invitation to take the Third Initiation in Eckankar—it was dated February 18, 2000.

I was now ready to explore the Causal Plane, the heaven where the records of our past lives are stored.

Football on the Beach

The Master had taken me for a visit to this plane of past-life memories four days after my Second Initiation in Eckankar. It was to let me know about the choices I had made concerning my present life.

Two possibilities were open to me to choose from. Would it be a life of material ease and comfort, or one of spiritual advancement?

The choice played out in a dream as beach football.

Beach of Life

As I stand with the Master on an expansive beach, an all-white group of American soccer players burst onto the beach with a ball and commence to organize play. The captain is female.

The Mahanta sends me a telepathic message: "Would

you like to join this team?"

I looked critically at the captain of the team. She has rather massive legs—almost as if she had elephantiasis. She would have problems being nimble in this game.

"Let me see the next team," I reply telepathically to the Mahanta.

Immediately, the white group disappears, and an all-black team bursts onto the beach with another soccer ball. The captain of this team is a slim, black male.

My eyes wander to his legs and feet. He is wearing Salvation Army boots.

"I'll join this team!" I tell the Mahanta.

At that, I promptly woke up in bed.

Later, in contemplation, I came to understand the dream.

I had been presented with two possible reincarnation choices based on my past-life karma. The team captains symbolized the bodies I was to choose between.

Choices

The first incarnation choice was that of a white female, a citizen of the United States, where I had lived as a white male in my last incarnation. The second possibility, which I finally chose, was that of the black male—my present body in Nigeria.

What was the reason for my choice?

Apparently, spiritual advancement, and not material ease, was my priority as Soul for this present life. The life of the white female, symbolized by her thick legs, was loaded with good karma. This good karma would allow little leeway for spiritual things. She would not be nimble on her "spiritual legs." In other words, she would be too well-heeled and weighed down with material goods to have much chance at advancing spiritually.

My Priority as Soul

This is not to say that rich, white, American women—or anybody, for that matter—can't make spiritual progress. This was an *individual* situation. Good karma or material goods might help others, in certain situations, advance spiritually. But in my case, it would have put me to sleep spiritually. I would have never met the Mahanta!

The black captain in my dream represented the body and circumstance that I finally chose.

Why did I choose the black captain?

His Salvation Army boots signified that this incarnation held the potential of spiritual liberation—the meeting with the Mahanta in this life!

Here, I want to mention some events in my youth that threatened to upset the apple cart, undermining my choice to reincarnate and meet the Mahanta in this life.

Early Marriage

As an impetuous twenty-three-year-old African, I met an equally impetuous twenty-one-year-old African-American. I'll call her Kay to protect her identity.

Kay had come from New York, where I'd been born in my last incarnation. She came for a six-month student-exchange program to the university I was attending in Nigeria. We met, and in a whirlwind courtship that lasted less than two months, we decided to get married!

She wrote her family back home, saying she had decided to marry this African dude. And her father responded with a word of caution: "Make sure he is not just using you to come to the States."

We had a good laugh over that one, because our problem was in the opposite direction—a groom who was reluctant to migrate to America!

I had been specific about our post-marriage place of abode. It was either Nigeria or there would be no marriage. Kay had agreed—for a while.

Refusal to Move

My reason for refusing to go to America had a spiritual basis. But it would take twenty years for me to discover it. Meanwhile my reason for refusing to leave Nigeria had to do with my family and community ties here.

My poor parents had worked their fingers to the bone to see their only son through to a master's degree in architecture. Western university education was not a priority then in this community, and some wondered why my parents went through the torture to see me through it. But then there were also many good-hearted people in the community who supported my parents' efforts. The community had virtually adopted me. There were times when my parents' best efforts fell short. Then the whole community would chip in through a fund-raiser to cover the necessary fees.

Even before the end of my education, I had become a role model for the youth in our community. How could I wave good-bye to all these wonderful people and simply fly off to America without first contributing something to their lives?

Spiritual Suicide?

It was twenty years later, and four days after my Second Initiation, that I would learn the spiritual reason for my refusal to move.

If I had moved to the United States at the time, I would have once again come face-to-face with the good karma that awaited the "white captain" in my dream! I would be in the incarnation choice I had rejected.

A move to the United States of America in my youth

would have been spiritual suicide!

But that is exactly what Kay, out of human love, tried to have me do. She had promised to return to Nigeria after finishing her degree. But the tough living conditions in Nigeria were fresh in her memory.

"I am making preparations for you to move over here," she wrote, without preamble or prior discussion, a couple of months prior to her graduation. "After all, your architectural profession can be better advanced over here than in Nigeria!"

I couldn't believe I had read her words right when I got the letter.

Cultural Wedge

My main interest in life was not to advance my profession. My role in our community came first.

We were both young and inexperienced. And neither of us was even minutely aware of the spiritual realities that drove a wedge into our relationship. A heart-to-heart discussion could have done us a world of good. But how does one discuss something heart to heart across the Atlantic?

Instead, angry letters crisscrossed the Atlantic Ocean like intercontinental ballistic missiles. Two people from different cultures with different values were trying to salvage a relationship across ten thousand kilometers of salt water and were only succeeding in making each other madder.

The Call of Community

To Kay, our relationship was strictly like that of a pair of frogs during the mating season—just the two of us, with no third party, our private love song croaking on. The issue of community and parents did not have a croaking chance. To her, life was a good career, money, and material stuff.

My life was anchored in the love of a community that had brought me up. We were miles apart, both in space and values.

Phones were a rarity in Nigeria in those days. We had to wait for more than a month sometimes just to receive the next salvo of frustration from each other's letters. I don't recommend an epistolary marital disagreement over the Atlantic!

Not too long after the disagreement started, I got a letter from a lawyer in Harlem. The gist of it: "Your wife has asked us to file suit for a divorce. We have tried to dissuade her—blah blah blah—to no avail." It was one suit I would not—could not—defend against.

Only when I got into Eckankar did I discover that of all calls in life, the call of the Mahanta is the highest of all.

I wish I knew this fact then. It would have saved me much heartache and recrimination. But perhaps the lack of understanding and the resulting pain was part and parcel of the purification process—a process that would help me advance to the meeting with the Mahanta twenty or so years later.

Burglars

Some years ago when my home was burglarized, I wondered why the Mahanta allowed this to happen when we were already in a bad financial situation.

I discovered it was to let us put to rest a huge volume of karma, forgotten memories from way back in Atlantis. It was a kind of spiritual plea bargain!

Residential ECK Center

When nobody in Gboko would rent his place to be used as an ECK center, I asked, as a last resort, that the ECK center move into my rented residence. There, it took up valuable space in the living room. Furthermore, when it came time to host a regional seminar and we could not afford to hire a hotel, we once more turned to our "residential ECK center."

Two days after that seminar, our living-room-cum-ECK-center was burglarized!

Ours was perhaps the poorest residence on the block. Why did the burglars choose us and not one of our richer neighbors?

Creative Artists

Two days before the burglary, I had a dream about it without recognizing the symbols.

In this dream, the seminar creative-arts performers, who came from outside our local area, return. They left a few things behind, and they have come to retrieve them.

On the night of the break-in, my wife Soul Traveled to the living room while the burglary was in progress! Frozen with fear, she could neither scream nor raise an alarm, even though she returned to her body and woke up when the burglars must have still been inside!

A Use for the Burglary

When day broke, we walked into our poorly furnished living-room-cum-ECK-center. If it was bad before, it was worse now.

The red rug, the only luxury in the room, had been removed, leaving exposed the stained cement floor. Someone had used a car jack to bend the protective iron bars on the street-side window, so as to gain access and to pull the looted property through the window.

Our curtains had been a mixed lot from the flea market. The burglars selected the best of them and left us those with holes in them. They also took an inexpensive wall clock that belonged to Eckankar. Symbolically the missing clock said time was up for working through this karma!

Another item the burglars took seemed like a strange choice to me at first but not later.

It was a sixteen-by-twenty-inch photograph of Sri Harold Klemp, the Mahanta, the Living ECK Master. Unknown to me at the time, it was a symbol to let us know that the Mahanta had a special use for this burglary!

Accused!

One of the youthful burglars was arrested the next day, trying to sell the rug, and the police then raided a drinking joint where the arrested youth said his accomplice was. But one policeman became ambitious; he tried to make the arrest alone, hoping to earn a promotion. And so the youth who had the curtain and the Master's picture as his share of the loot escaped arrest.

The case eventually went to court with that one youth as the accused. I was called as principal witness for the prosecution. After I made the first appearance, the Master brought me back to court in the dream state.

But whereas in the outer court I was witness for the prosecution, in the dream state I returned as the accused!

Kangaroo Court?

In the dream, I enter the court in company of the Mahanta who appears in the form of a close friend. Instead of the witness stand, I am called to the dock for the accused!

"Did this man (my companion) bring you to this court?" the prosecutor asks.

When I answer in the affirmative, he throws up his hands in great jubilation. The police and other court officials join in the jubilation. The lawyer runs out of

*the courtroom, to a group of lawyers outside waiting
their turn to come to court.*

*"He has pleaded guilty!" the lawyer exclaims before
his colleagues. Another round of jubilation echoes outside the court. Am I in court or a sports arena? What
kind of nonsense is this? Is it some kind of kangaroo
court? I wonder.*

*I look helplessly at the judge, who, unknown to me,
is one of the Lords of Karma. He simply shrugs as if to
say, "Well, that's it; if this man brought you here, that's
the verdict!"*

As the judge prepared to write down the judgment,
I woke up in bed, terribly upset.

"What was that all about?" I asked the Mahanta in
contemplation.

"It could have been worse," he said.

Noah's Ark

Another night in a dream, I was given an incredibly
fat volume of a book, fatter than a single-volume ency-
clopedia. It was titled *The Untold Story of Noah's Ark*.
Before I could read it, I woke up.

From my contemplations, other follow-up dreams,
and Soul Travel experiences, I discovered that *The
Untold Story of Noah's Ark* was the record of karmic
debts I had incurred as a high-court judge in ancient
Atlantis (whose deluge-and-destruction story later became known in traditional religions as the Flood).

Justice to the Highest Bidder

This story began to unfold during several Soul Travel
trips with the Master into Atlantis, with its extremely
wet, smoggy climate. I discovered that I had not only
wronged the two youthful burglars, but the karmic-
debt chain I had caused involved the judge in the present
case, as well as police investigators, the prosecution

lawyer, and a lot of other court officials. The lawyers outside the courtroom in my dream were people not directly involved in the present case; yet they were waiting to prosecute me for other, similar cases!

As high-court judge back in Atlantis, I more often than not sold justice to the highest bidder. In one case, two or more families were fighting over rich mines of precious stones on the side of a mountain. The winds of justice kept shifting as the opposing parties brought money to me at night. It was in my interest for the case to drag on as long as possible.

The long line of people waiting to prosecute me was impressive. The guilty plea the Master made on my behalf turned out to be a generous plea bargain, as all these cases against me were now being prosecuted concurrently in the dream state!

I withdrew as witness from the case on the outer. I learned later that the burglar was discharged for lack of diligent prosecution. But in the dream state, I continued to come to court to be prosecuted.

Atlantean Karma Straightened Out

One night in the dream state, I came to court and found that the short, crooked road that passed by the court premises on the outer had now been reconstructed. The curbing was so straight, it took my breath away. This was an indication that the voluminous tangle of Atlantean karma had been straightened out at last.

The last appearance I made in court as the accused took place in the presence of my present wife and in-laws. The judge struck with his gavel and got up, and we all stood up. He bent down and kissed the table. Then he took all the files of my Atlantis court karma, put them in strong, circular aluminum cases, and carried them out of court into the sunshine. We followed.

Outside, he opened a deep well, dropped the cases

into it, and sealed the top with a tight-fitting concrete stopper.

After that, I never appeared in court again in the dream state.

One day, however, a policeman came to me on the inner planes. "Come and retrieve your rug," he said.

A few days later, on the outer, an emissary came from the police and invited me to go and recover my stolen rug. The curtains and the Master's photograph have never been recovered, as of the time of this writing. I hope the picture does the burglar some good.

It was enlightening to see how the inner justice system always got their man—even if it took many lifetimes.

I may not be a lawyer or judge in this lifetime (in fact, perhaps because of this karma, I have always been uncomfortable with the legal profession in this life), but I am now in a position to appreciate true justice from which no misdeed is exempt!

The Accident That Failed

The dreamer's inner life begins to straighten out once he takes up the study of ECK. The arena of the dreamer's subtle worlds is graced by the entrance of the Mahanta, who erases karmic burdens through the creative use of dreams.

—Sri Harold Klemp,
The Art of Spiritual Dreaming[2]

Both ECKists and non-ECKists suffer and enjoy the effects of their karma. But only the student of the Mahanta sometimes gets his karma resolved in the dream state, reducing the wear and tear of having to go through it all physically.

Fatal Accident

I was about three years short of meeting the Mahanta, when I was involved in a fatal accident.

A youthful stowaway in a dump truck carrying sand from the river jumped off as the vehicle was turning in to tip its load. I did not see him at first, as a passing vehicle concealed his mad dash into the road. The concrete median in the express road prevented me from swinging my car left to avoid him in the split second that I did see him.

Five days later, he died in the intensive-care unit at the hospital. I was heartbroken. Why did this needless accident happen?

It was only years later, after I had been in Eckankar for a while, that I discovered this fellow whom I'd hit had killed me in a past life. And, by the inflexible laws of karma, I was compelled to balance the books. Since I had no ill intentions for anybody in this life, the Lords of Karma found this creative way to compel both of us via an "offer we couldn't refuse" to balance the books of past-life karma. Before meeting the Mahanta, it's always an eye for an eye and a tooth for a tooth, whether we choose it or not.

Yet Again

Then I became an ECKist. I did not know it at the time, but the Lords of Karma were about to present another creative "balancing of the books" with another of my murderers from a past life.

I got a preview of this impending accident in the dream state. I'd also previewed the first accident this way, but that dream from my pre-ECK days was fuzzy. In this second case, the Master provided a rather delightful and unusual dream which showed with perfect clarity how this new accident would happen. But the forewarning was lost on me at first, because the experience was so silly that I did not regard it as anything serious.

Forewarning

In this Soul Travel experience in the dream state, I was driving to Gboko from Makurdi at a fast pace. At kilometer eighteen, the accident of a few years before was about to repeat itself.

A ten-year-old boy sprinted into the road from my left side. Short of my committing suicide by swinging into the bush at one hundred and forty kilometers (eighty-seven miles) an hour, we would collide. But in the dream, I had an alternative.

I surprised myself by putting my leg through the side window and stretching it like a telescopic antenna. I hooked my foot under the boy's armpit and threw him back to where he had come from. That way, I avoided the collision.

When I woke up, I laughed till my sides hurt. I shared the dream with a friend who shares my sense of humor, and we had a good laugh over it.

Nothing serious here, I thought, *just one of the quaint jokes of the dream worlds.*

I was wrong!

Almost nine months after that inner experience, it happened on the outer!

I was late for an ECK program in Gboko, and I was pushing the speed limit. I must have been whipping along at perhaps one hundred and forty kilometers an hour, when—at exactly kilometer eighteen, like in the dream—a boy of about ten ran out from behind a parked minibus into the road. In another instant, we would meet in a collision of flesh and metal.

Laws of Physics Bypassed?

Oh, no! was my first thought. *Not again!*

The people watching from the roadside did not even have time to scream. The movement of my foot from the accelerator to the brake pedal was only an involuntary reaction born of years of driving. By the laws of physics, it was a useless gesture. I closed my eyes, not wishing to witness the collision.

I heard and felt nothing!

What happened—or rather, didn't happen?

I opened my eyes and looked in the rearview mirror. A pair of bare pink feet was flashing into the savanna grass on the right side of the road! The young fellow and my car had just passed through the same spot without colliding!

If my dream of forewarning nearly nine months earlier had not been so utterly wild, I might not have recalled it much less connected it with the event that had just occurred.

Stretching Time

Some time later, I read that the ECK Masters, in their work, have the power to stretch, shorten, or stop the perception of time if necessary to provide protection. Only then did this dream and outer experience begin to make sense.

Via the scene of my stretching a telescoping leg through the window to save the child in the dream, the Master was telling me that I would one day witness and benefit from the Master's ability to stretch time and alter fate.

The Lords of Karma had wanted to balance a karmic debt that was more a nuisance than a lesson for me in the present. The Master let me bypass this useless event.

Granted, the other fellow was probably still under the strict hand of fate; but I was not anymore. He would have to look for another if he was serious about dying at such a young age.

This was one of the most dramatic and incredible experiences in my life. Even today, it feels as if it happened to someone else.

Balustrade

Circumstances brought Torbunde (not his real name) and I together. We became like brothers. I trusted him, and he trusted me. We belonged to different religions and had different social and economic backgrounds, but this did not get in the way of our friendship, which was based on mutual respect and trust.

Torbunde was a hard-working man, but for some strange reason, he could not take charge of his life. He did not know how to charge fees for the professional services that he often rendered others. And so he lived in penury.

If anyone gave Torbunde an assignment, he rarely failed. Yet, for some reason he could not duplicate such action to initiate and do things with his considerable energies to better his own lot. So ruthless people often took advantage of him, without doing anything for him in return. It was a strange karmic condition.

Plunge to Certain Death

One day, I sat in contemplation. In full consciousness, I went out of the body. I was looking down at the flat roof of a high-rise building. On the top of this building stood Torbunde. As I looked on, a powerful wind that turned into a tornado began to blow. It began to carry Torbunde toward the edge of the building's roof that had no guardrails.

Torbunde went flat on his belly and tried to clutch at anything he could hold on to, to avoid the plunge to certain death. It was no good.

Imagination

I knew that I was in the Soul body and that this ethereal form was useless for grabbing Torbunde and hauling him to safety. "What can I do?" I asked as I helplessly watched my friend about to fall to his death.

"You've got imagination," the Mahanta whispered in my inner being.

As Torbunde slid closer to the edge, I began to imagine a strong iron railing at the rim of the flat roof. For a while, nothing happened. I wondered whether I had failed.

However, when Torbunde reached the edge of the roof and was about to fall off, a strong, black, metal railing sprouted into place—just in time. Now safe, he hung on to the railing, panting. Then I came awake.

Medical Bills

Some years down the road, Torbunde began to get a series of different illnesses. There were several times when the doctors doubted he would make it. By now, I understood what that Soul Travel experience had been all about. But I had this assurance—he would somehow pull through.

In time, the doctors diagnosed the cause of his illnesses. But it was not something that could be cured with one medical treatment or prescription. He would probably require endless medical attention for the rest of his life.

Torbunde had more or less lived the life of a drifter, so he could not afford these costs. And the medical bills fell to me.

In the dream state, the Master also showed me a worse scenario. If Torbunde translated (died), the upkeep and care of his family would become fully my lot!

Selfless Love

One evening, I asked the Mahanta for an insight into this relationship. I wanted to understand why the cost of Torbunde's health care, and even the care of his family, became my lot.

The Master took me back to a lifetime when *I* was the drifter. I had no loved ones of any kind in my life, and hence no support. Torbunde and his spouse—also his wife in this life—took me in and cared for me as if I was one of their own.

They had absolutely nothing to gain, except the ridicule of their neighbors, for housing such a vagrant. But that did not bother them in the slightest.

Torbunde had been willing to share everything. It was selfless love.

The good karma he created for himself, by giving love with no expectations of getting anything back, had paid off for him in this life. And I was also being given the chance, under the Master's guidance, to return this love that had been given to me selflessly in the past when I needed it most.

Torbunde is not an ECKist, yet a love bond existed between us. The Master helped me, via Soul Travel and other means, to give assistance to this fellow Soul in need. Now Torbunde has more days to pursue his spiritual goals in this life.

Casual Friendship

I used to meet Sylvester at the mechanics village in Makurdi, capital of Benue State in central Nigeria. We both had Volkswagens, so we used the same mechanics.

There was an easy, spontaneous camaraderie between us, though we didn't become real friends. I liked him, and he liked me, and that was it. However, the Mahanta showed me why it was worthwhile for me to better understand this easy relationship.

Arrest

I had the following dream, which was obviously about a past life.

Sylvester is a policeman. I am wanted by the authorities. I have no idea for what reason. Sylvester has been sent to bring me in.

Perhaps he is sure I am not guilty, or perhaps he just likes me. He has met me in the house where I live.

"Get out, and get as far away from here as you can,"
he advises.

I take off.

On another day, I am walking on the streets. I once more run into Sylvester in his police uniform. I am still a wanted man. Yet, Sylvester keeps a straight face, pretends not to see me, and walks on by.

This dream was one of those snippets of information one gets in the dream world to explain the exotic or mundane experiences of life. They can be quite educational.

Why We Like Each Other

When I meet Sylvester at the mechanic's, we just enjoy each other's company. He doesn't know the reason for this easy camaraderie between us. Now I do. Unfortunately, this is one snippet of information I cannot share with him.

Sylvester belongs to a belief system which teaches

that man lives but once. Afterward comes judgment and a permanent trip to either heaven or hell.

However, our casual friendship endures in spite of the bleak gospel of his church. And I'm glad to have caught a glimpse of the past-life connection behind it.

If the Master, on some later date or perhaps in another lifetime, wants Sylvester to know why we have this easy but distant relationship, it shall be so. But for now, it's enough that the camaraderie we share enhances both our lives.

The Bone Shall Return

I called her the Bone because she had very little flesh on her body. She might have been five feet—one and a half meters—tall or less. She tipped the scales at just forty-five kilograms—less than a hundred pounds. She was a friend from many lifetimes, as I discovered in my dreams and contemplations.

But my wife somehow never liked the Bone, and she did not hide that fact.

Baba

One day I visited the Bone, who was a single parent to a daughter.

"You know this man's name?" she asked her daughter. When the daughter shook her head, she said, "This man is Baba—Baba of the Bone." From that day on, till she translated (died) years later, the Bone called me by that name—Baba of the Bone.

After the Bone translated, we often met in the other worlds. There she was still undergoing treatment at the hospital for the illness she had died of.

One day, I met the Bone in contemplation as I sat singing HU. She stood before me, looking radiant. Her illness was now gone. She smiled that special smile of hers, with her pointed incisors showing, just like she'd do on the physical when really amused. Then the Bone disappeared.

Not Satisfied with One Outing

On another day, I had an outing in the inner worlds with the Bone and a friend who was actually the Mahanta in disguise.

"Let's drop the Bone at her place," I said to the Mahanta.

I did not know it then, but I was requesting that our karmic relationship from past lives come to an end.

The Bone punched me playfully in the stomach. "I am not satisfied with this outing," she said.

A week later, the Bone confirmed that she had won a "court case" against me. We would have another "outing."

In the dream state, I had filed a divorce suit, asking for separation from the Bone. We met, and she informed me that she had successfully appealed against the divorce. "You'll get a life sentence," she said, laughing so hard her ribs might crack. "I wonder how you'll be any good to me when serving life imprisonment." She was really shaking with laughter now.

Through the Back Door

My wife was on the pill, and her cycle was often erratic. When her monthly rhythm failed, she assured me it was nothing.

"I don't have the usual signs of pregnancy," she said.

Two months—no period, no morning sickness.

Three months—still no period and no morning sickness, nor any other signs of conception. Now wondering, she decided to check with our family doctor.

"Madam," the doctor said, adjusting his stethoscope, "you are three months pregnant."

"What are you going to do about it?" I asked her later.

"Whoever it is sneaked in through the back door, and I might as well let him or her in," she said with humor. Then both of us began to wonder who had sneaked in, in this fashion. What Soul wanted to join our family?

Who Is It?

One Saturday, I traveled to Otukpo from Gboko for an ECK Worship Service the next day. The Peugeot taxi I rode in had four people, including the driver, in the front seat, packed tighter than sardines. We were getting the special service of the Nigerian National Union of Road Transport Workers.

In concern for life, limb, and comfort, I went into contemplation and asked the Master for succor. I wanted to be in good condition to receive the new member that was about to join our family.

"By the way," I asked the Master as I went into contemplation, "who is it?"

I must have gone at it rather well, because soon, even in such cramped conditions, I fell asleep. Then the vehicle jerked suddenly to a crawl at a bad patch in the road, waking me. I peered through the windshield into the night.

A large form loomed before my eyes. Our driver had almost run into the back of a very big truck that had also slowed down at the bad patch of road. There was some writing on the tailgate of the truck. The night was dark, but then we were also pretty close.

I almost burst into laughter when I read the message. It was the answer to the question I had asked before going into contemplation.

The writing on the tailgate read The Bone Shall Return!

Mixed Feelings

When I returned from Otukpo, my wife told me of an experience she'd had some time ago.

She was at an ECK regional seminar. When she opened the door to the children's room, the Bone was staring at her from the opposite side of the room.

Am I not yet rid of this person? she'd thought. *I'd heard she'd left Eckankar. What is she doing here in the children's room?*

The Bone was once enrolled in Eckankar. But after receiving the ECK discourses for a year, her life got complicated and she dropped out.

While the Bone was active in Eckankar, she'd shared a dream with me. We were going on a journey, and we came to a large stream. She could not continue, because she was afraid of the water. She said I then picked her up and hurled her across the stream onto a thatched hut. She crashed through the roof and fell on the bed inside, unharmed.

I've since thought her dream might indicate that somehow I would become an instrument to help her connect with the ECK teachings once more.

Hand of Fate Softened

A few days after my return from Otukpo, my wife delivered a baby girl. Somehow, without knowing why, she decided to be "baby friendly" for this particular child, which meant only breast milk—no food or water—for six months! It was a crushing and limiting schedule. But no one had imposed it on her. And she saw it through! Perhaps it was her way of ending the negative karma between them that made her not like the Bone in the past.

And probably because of that wonderful start in life, this girl has been the healthiest child in our family. She also has the closest bond with her mother.

Two people who cared little for each other have turned out to be the closest allies.

The hand of fate has been softened for them too!

Baba Once Again

All my children have called me Dad since the first one started the fashion.

Not the Bone.

When this girl started to talk, a year after she was born, instead of imitating her senior siblings, she started calling me Baba! If she had not been so limited in speech, I believe she would have added "of the Bone"!

But she had done enough to confirm her identity. The Bone had indeed returned!

Try this spiritual exercise today!

— ⁂ —

Formula Three Technique

Formula Three works for visiting the Causal Plane. This is the plane of seed ideas and seed karma and of past-life memories.

First, record in your dream journal that you are trying this technique.

Chant HU three times, then breathe three times. You keep doing this for fifteen minutes, before bed or in contemplation. Lightly keep in mind that you want to visit the Causal Plane.

When you go to sleep, you very gently try to hold thoughts of the Causal Plane.

Note and record your dreams.

You might begin to get revelations from your past lives!

—Adapted from "The Formula Technique" in *The Spiritual Exercises of ECK* by Harold Klemp[3]

6

Mind over Matter

If man depends upon thought alone he will be most unhappy, because thought and intelligence only lead to unhappiness. Mind, consciousness, and intelligence are the ruling factors upon this plane. The outward manifestation of these three is thought, which so often becomes confused when trying to analyze the works of ECK, or what could be called the chewing of the mental processes on some parts of the ECK works.

—*The Shariyat-Ki-Sugmad*, Books One & Two[1]

The following dream concerned my inaugural movement into the fourth plane, the Mental Plane, the origin of the computer and thoughts in general.

Computer Country

I amble into an office for an inaugural computer course. The office has many computers supervised by Chinese- or Japanese-looking people.

I arrive late. I had been given some long computer printouts earlier, but I had at first discarded them because I thought they were of no consequence. Then I dis-

117

covered that all the information I needed for this class was on the discarded printouts. It is because I had been sorting all this out that I arrive late to this place where a lecture is now in progress. The teacher, a wealthy colleague of mine, looks at me with distaste as I walk in late, but he says nothing. When I am shown to my seat, I find it to be quite comfortable. In spite of that, I sit in this class in a very disoriented state of mind.

Predictions

This dream predicted a number of things.

I had arrived later than expected at this level of heaven.

Some of my dreams in the past had predicted that I might not take the Fourth Initiation on the outer—perhaps because I had thought those computer printouts (Mental-Plane lessons) were not important. It was a warning not to ignore the experiences at this level!

What long computer printouts!

The wealthy colleague was the Mahanta in disguise.

This is the level at which I would finally have to work through an overbalance of accumulated good karma. The comfortable seat predicted comfortable outer circumstances here. But when I began to have dream experiences on this plane, they were often confused and garbled—very unlike my earlier clear dreams.

Several Important Steps

Five days later in the dream state, the computer course came to an end.

"That was quick!" I wrote in my dream journal.

However, five days' gap between the two dreams translated into a five-year gap on the outer!

Earlier dreams had predicted several important steps for me at this level of life. And the possibility that no outer initiation would confirm my arrival in the Fourth Plane at first riled and concerned me. How would I be prepared to meet the circumstances here?

The Shariyat-Ki-Sugmad says this of the initiate at this level:

> Man's perceptions on any concept which is beyond him develops into trust and faith that all will be well provided. He will leave the ECK alone and let It work in him to grow into the mighty stream, which It assuredly will, in time. This is the development of the progressive knowledge of the Sugmad [God]; it will create the illusions of problems because man will not want to turn from his acquired knowledge, gained from books and discourses, to enter into the full trust of his inner senses. He wants to let himself argue and chew mentally over the aspects of the illusions, creating damage to his faith, his health, and his thinking process.[2]

Very reassuring, when one of the experiences I was expected to have while here was meeting the Angel of Death!

Angel of Death

Little by little, the Mahanta began to let me know via dreams that I was about to face situations in my health that could lead to death.

I'm standing on a cliff, and I have a copy of The Shariyat-Ki-Sugmad, *Book One, in my breast pocket. As I bend over to peer down at the river below, the book slides out and falls into the water. I am surprised at how strong the current is. The book is swept out of sight at once.*

A single, long log bridges the river, and I cross to the other side, hanging under the log like a sloth.

After I cross, I run downstream. I think there is a bend in the river where I can wait for the book and recover it. However, when I get there, the expected bend in the river is nowhere in sight.

"Go to Onitsha," an impression tells me, "and you will meet the river once more."

In this dream, the copy of *The Shariyat-Ki-Sugmad*, Book One, that had fallen in the river symbolized my physical body and its probable demise.

The expected bend in the river was the Causal Plane. Onitsha, a riverside town in Nigeria, symbolized the Mental Plane.

In many of my dreams, my car would symbolize my physical body. In one dream, my car also went over the cliff and into a river.

Car over the Bridge

My cousin is struggling with my Santana saloon car (sedan) near the far end of an old bridge. Behind the car, on the bridge, sits a thirty-seater bus, and behind the bus is a truck.

When did he learn to drive? *I wonder, deeply worried. Then, as I expected, he loses control of the vehicle, and it rolls over into the drink.*

I rush over and look into the churning waters of the river from the steep cliff.

I see that a friend of mine, who translated (died) four days earlier, is now down there in the river. He has grabbed the car by the rear bumper and is barely keeping it afloat.

"Don't let go, please!" I beg. "I am going to get help to fish that car out."

The words are hardly out of my mouth, when his fingers lose their hold and the car sinks. Weakly, my deceased friend begins to swim downstream in the strong current. The bus and the truck slowly back up.

I run over the bridge and head to where there is a bend in the river. As I run through the forest, I encounter mountains upon mountains of human waste—a symbol of the huge amount of karma from the lower Astral Plane that I need to work through concerning my health. The river has now completely disappeared underground. Only a large hole provides a peephole into the water below. The river waters finally burst out into a dam. My deceased friend now lies resignedly on the dam's retaining wall. He has given up and surrendered to death.

Inside, I know that if my car reaches that dam, I will have to kiss it good-bye.

When I woke up, I understood the dream clearly.

The car represented my physical body. I was about to lose it.

The bus and the truck were my emotional (Astral) and memory (Causal) bodies respectively. Once the physical body was lost in death, they would retract back across the "bridge" that separates the physical from the subtle planes. The car getting to the "dam" represented physical death.

Contemplation

My only hope to salvage this situation lay in the Spiritual Exercises of ECK. I therefore went into contemplation and began to use Soul's mock-ups.

I dialed the Mahanta using a cell phone and explained the situation to him. In my imagination, he arrived in a helicopter, which hovered over the river and dropped down a powerful cable, the end of which held a mechanical hand whose telescopic fingers could spread open from bank to bank. It had an electronic trigger, which a large object like a car would trip, causing the hand to clasp the object automatically.

The hand stayed in the water for a while, it was triggered and it began to be winched up by the cable. The car appeared inside the giant hand, and I cheered. The chopper flew over to a workshop by the river. ECK Master Yaubl Sacabi owned the workshop.

The vehicle was first dried out using powerful air jets. Then the repair work followed.

After it had been fixed, the car was returned to its place on the bridge. It once more led the way, and the bus (Astral body) and truck (Causal body) were reconnected to it in series with a strong silver chain (the silver cord). Then I drove the car across the bridge to physical life.

Wheel of Awagawan

Whenever the Master let me see another angle of my coming demise in any way, I would counter the pending disaster with a special spiritual exercise.

Some of these prophetic insights came in the form of a waking dream, a special spiritual message that showed up in the events of everyday life.

One evening, for example, I was driving up a steep, deserted road to a housing estate a short distance out of town. A friend of mine, who is built like the Mahanta, rode as a front-seat passenger.

As we drew close to a cottage hospital, a single bicycle tire came spinning down the road toward us. I stopped at the hospital and gave the tire lots of leeway to pass on to wherever it was headed. Instead, it suddenly wobbled, turned ninety degrees, went a short distance into the bush on the roadside, and then rolled back and crashed in the dirt road.

We sat silently in the car, wondering at this phenomenon.

We drove up the road, expecting to see a child who

might have played such a prank. We found no one. In fact no compound was even close by.

Our visit up the road lasted about an hour. But when we drove back along the same road, we found the bicycle tire still in the road, unclaimed. I drove past the tire and went home.

When I recorded this waking dream in my dream journal, I called it The Wheel of Awagawan, the wheel of life.

A week later, the Mahanta backed up this waking dream with a night dream to help me understand what was afoot.

Out of Fuel

In the dream, it was now my friend who drove, while I was the passenger. The Mahanta was letting me know that he was the driver of my life. There was nothing to worry about.

As we get to the brow of a hill, from where the road leads downhill then up to where we had encountered the bicycle tire by the cottage hospital, an irate woman stops us.

"Abacha (former military head of state who, four years after this dream, died in office) *is going to see trouble," she says, gesticulating. "We will go to town and stir up trouble. Wait till you see and hear the results."*

When we try to drive on, the engine of the car cuts out.

"It's the fuel," I tell my friend and driver. "I am surprised it lasted so long."

My friend eases the gearshift into neutral. Using gravity and the steep incline, we coast down, then up, and we swing onto the grounds of the cottage hospital and park. I pull out sixty naira—a large sum in the dream—and give the money to my companion.

"Twenty naira is for your fare for a bike," I say, "and forty naira is for the purchase of fuel for the car."

I wait beside a mound of earth (I would identify it in contemplation later as my grave, if I did not make it). *On this mound, I find a large bunch of keys. A lady soon appears, breathless. The lost keys are hers. She takes them from me and shows lots of gratitude.*

Upon awakening, the symbols in the dream became clear during contemplation.

The woman's tirade about the coming troubles for the head of state were Golden-tongued Wisdom, a form of prophecy, about my coming health crisis. The car being out of gas meant the life force that drove my physical body was running out. The hospital was an image of death and of hope at the same time—a place to die or to heal, depending on how I used the keys (Spiritual Exercises of ECK) that I found on my would-be grave in the dream.

Later, I also discovered that the money I provided for the bike fare and fuel purchase represented the good karma that awaited me at this level of life. By giving it to my companion (the Mahanta), I was giving him permission to use this store of good karma toward my healing process when the need arose.

Physical Signs of Illness

Physical signs of serious illness began to crop up about a year or two later. I began to lose weight steadily. Very soon, my muscular atrophy was so bad that hardly any flesh stood between my fingers and my tibia when I held my shins.

I stayed indoors and took walks—when my legs could carry me—only at night, to avoid public speculations on my state of health.

Convulsive fevers and chills began to hit me now

and then, and my blood pressure went through the roof. When my ankles enlarged due to edema, I knew that my internal organs were likely failing in their job.

The natural solution would have been to go to a good doctor. But where was the money? I had hit one of the lowest financial points in my life, and I had no means with which to seek medical support. All I could look to was the Mahanta and the Spiritual Exercises of ECK.

Sometimes ECKists in the Western world wonder why ECKists in Africa have such a strong trust in the Mahanta. I discovered the answer at this period in my life.

The Mahanta once told a story about a schoolteacher who noticed that one student was always using a black crayon to color every work of his. The teacher wondered if there was something wrong with the boy. But when the school psychologist had a tête-à-tête with this student, he discovered the simple truth: the black crayon was the only crayon the student possessed![3]

It is often like this with the ECKists in Africa. There may be no stable government, reliable law courts, good economy, or even medical facilities that he or she can lean upon. Often, the only "crayon" the ECKist in Africa has to paint life with is the Mahanta! I know, because I was now at that point in the road.

White Cat

As my health went downhill, a little drama took place in my house.

A white cat with a single black patch on its flank followed me one evening as I walked into our family compound. Later, I would consider this female cat, which took up residence in our compound, to be a spiritual entity sent to ensure that I survived my coming ordeal.

But I did not know this at the time.

From day one, the cat behaved as if she had always been there with us.

Since I rarely went out in the daytime, the white cat always stayed in bed with me throughout the day. At night, she would go out to hunt. Then she would return in the morning, slip into my bedroom, and lie with her head nuzzling my feet, purring contentedly.

One day this cat, without any prior evidence of a problem, suddenly went into convulsions. With a blood-curdling scream, she went into a spin like a whirling dervish and then collapsed.

At first I was devastated. Would she die just like that?

She didn't. Apparently, she still had some of her nine lives left. The cat recovered after about an hour and showed no sign of her recent health crisis.

I have often wondered in hindsight—did this cat take on part of my karmic load during this episode to lighten the weight for me?

After being with us for a while, the cat became pregnant. Still she kept up her habit of going out to hunt at night and returning in the morning to lie quietly nuzzling my feet.

One morning, the cat returned from her hunt. But instead of lying down and nuzzling my feet, the cat, for the first time, came up and lay curled in my armpit.

I was half asleep when I realized that the cat was making strange movements. When I got up to investigate, I discovered that not only was the cat in labor, but one of the kittens was already emerging from her body!

I jumped up and took the cat to a proper place for delivery.

She produced three kittens.

Several days later, upon returning from a trip to Abuja, Nigeria's federal capital, my children told me that the mother cat, while in the process of nursing the kittens, had died. Her ninth life was apparently spent.

Now I was left with three six-day-old kittens. How could I help them make it to adulthood?

Fight for Life

I bought the milk I could afford. Infant formula was beyond my financial reach. But the biggest problem was how to get the milk into those tiny mouths.

I stumbled upon an idea—a syringe! I didn't think of it at the time, but I would later realize there was a powerful healing image associated with the syringe.

So with a syringe, I tried as best I could to feed the kittens. But within one week, all three kittens sadly passed away, one after the other.

"What was all that about?" I asked the Inner Master.

It suddenly occurred to me that while I was busy trying to help the kittens survive, my mind was taken off my health condition and the possibility of my death. Perhaps this shift of attention from my condition to the survival of something other than myself did some good.

Of course, the kittens died in the end, and it's hard to see the good in that. Could these Souls in kitten bodies have accepted part of my karma and given of themselves—even their lives? Who can say? Yet, while they lived, they helped me focus on healing.

I needed this focus, because I was soon to meet the Angel of Death and face a decision on whether I would remain in a physical body or not.

Wrestling Match

One night, on my way to the Mental Plane, I saw ECK Master Wu Tenna walking behind me. This ECK Master now works as the spiritual head of the Temple of Golden Wisdom on the Mental Plane.[4]

I had read about another ECKist's inner experience with him tying back to an incarnation on Jupiter some four million years ago.[5] His description of Wu Tenna can be politely described as very interesting. To me he looked tall and very angular.

Walking along the road, I found someone lying languorously across our path, facedown. His head seemed to be covered with a hood, reminding me of a wrestler called the Undertaker.

I am surprised that I did not recoil when the man lying in the road turned his head. He appeared to be a normal human being—up to his neck. But his face was a skull with absolutely no flesh on it!

I did not know it, but I was now face-to-face with the Angel of Death.

"It's not possible to continue with your journey," he said in a flat, matter-of-fact, perhaps even bored tone of voice. He'd said that to billions before me. Why should my case excite him?

I ignored him and tried to pass, but he sprang up with agility a monkey would have envied. Then a wrestling match ensued between us.

The Angel of Death was easy to throw. The problem was, every time I threw him and tried to get up, he immediately sprang up, sticking to me like a burr.

All this time, while I wrestled the Angel of Death, Wu Tenna stood chuckling. Then, with the greatest kindness, he took me by the shoulder, still chuckling, and drew me back from my wrestling embrace with the Angel of Death.

"The Angel of Death is a difficult adversary to floor," he said via the inner channels. Wu Tenna then showed me a secret bypath the Angel of Death had not covered with his body, and we continued our journey to the Mental Plane.

Out here on the physical, I still had many battles to fight before I would find that secret path around the Angel of Death.

My health was perhaps in its deepest trouble in 1997. It would be several years before I'd begin to move away from the wrestling match with the Angel of Death. Yet, eventually, after major surgery, my health would begin to improve.

Survival Kit

First, my car suffered from two engine knocks in quick succession. And my physical body looked like it might also suffer "engine knock" at any time.

It was as if the Mahanta had used part of the "sixty naira" I'd given him in the dream related earlier to "purchase more fuel" to help me run my body so it didn't quit. He bought insurance coverage from my repository of good karma to help prolong my stay in the physical body.

The sole reason for helping prolong my stay in the body was to let me take another step up the spiritual mountain. I had both the potential and enthusiasm to do this. It would have been such a waste of time to translate (die), reincarnate, and then have to pick up the trail to find the Mahanta all over again.

At least thrice over a period of three or more years, the Mahanta came to offer specific medicinal help. He recommended the root of an herb similar to sarsaparilla to help me get my health together. I added this to my survival kit.

Clinic on the Inner

Another method the Mahanta used was to take me in the Soul body to an inner-world clinic. There I encountered technology that is not in common use here on earth.

The inner-world clinic has a cell-cloning facility.

Huge refrigerators hold frozen crustaceans, which exhibit life and movement even in their frozen condition.

Another piece of equipment here is like a cyclotron. It is used for the cell cloning.

Old or sick cells are bathed in a reagent to soften the cell walls. Next, nuclei are extracted from the crustaceans and fired like bullets at the sick or old cells.

If the nuclei are fired at a certain precise speed, they knock out the bad nuclei from the cells on impact. The nuclei used as projectiles, having penetrated the weakened cells and displaced the diseased nuclei, then lodge inside the cells.

Maybe it is the shock of the impact, or maybe there is an electric charge, or there could be some other reason—but each cell with its new nucleus begins to behave as if it was fertilized. It begins dividing rapidly, producing new healthy cells.

Once implanted inside a damaged organ, the new healthy cells grow rapidly and take over the functions of the old, dying cells in the organ. In the end, the whole organ regenerates.

I wonder if perhaps crustaceans were chosen as stem cells because all life is said to have come from the sea.

The lab attendants leave me to try my hand at this methodology for a while. My early efforts are quite messy, but as time goes on, I start to become adept at the technique.

Then I awoke in bed.

I had goose pimples from my neck down my torso like someone with German measles. These goose pimples stayed with me for about a month.

The edema in my legs, feet, and ankles began to gradually recede. Soon, it disappeared completely. My health began to improve dramatically, and it has continued to improve right up to the time of this writing!

Doubting-Thomas Syndrome

Why do we become doubting Thomases?

It is the mind that doubts. Soul lives beyond the mind. And the two often clash, creating conflict within the individual. The poor physical apparatus is then torn: will it be directed by the real self, Soul; or the mind, which doubts everything it cannot contain? We often get into spiritual trouble when the mind wins the battle over Soul in commanding the attention of the physical. When the mind, which should be the servant, becomes the master, trouble comes!

In my early days of membership in Eckankar, someone sent me a book and a message. The man belonged to a religious teaching with origins in India.

"Eckankar is a breakaway sect of the real thing," his note said. "Why would you be satisfied with a broken branch instead of the main tree?"

Who Copied Whom?

It seems the author of the book had traveled to India and met a guru. And the teachings of this guru were the substance of the book.

That alone was not unsettling. What was, was the discovery that sometimes, for several continuous pages, this book and Paul Twitchell's *Spiritual Notebook* appeared to match each other almost word for word! The most noticeable difference between Paul Twitchell's book and the other was that the latter advocated vegetarianism and abstinence from sex as a recipe for spirituality, while Paul had none of that in his teachings.

Now, this other book was first published in 1939. Paul Twitchell published his *Spiritual Notebook* sometime after 1965, when he became the Mahanta, the

Living ECK Master. On this account alone, it was hard not to speculate about who copied whom.

What was going on here? Had Paul Twitchell copied from this other book when he wrote *The Spiritual Notebook*?

Faith in ECK Rocked

I sat down for a long time and wondered about all this. My faith in the teachings of Eckankar was being badly rocked.

I looked the matter over, and I knew I had to come to some decision.

The first thing I did was to reflect on my past experiences that had brought me into Eckankar and weigh the spiritual experiences I was still having as an ECKist.

I recalled the series of pre-ECK experiences that had sensitized me to these teachings before I encountered them. I looked at all the inner invitations and subsequent experiences that had brought me into Eckankar, including the Lagos experience where the Inner Master had appeared and I had stepped forward. I also recalled that the form of the Inner Master I had encountered looked like that of Harold Klemp (whom I saw only later on the outer) and nothing like any of the Indian gurus whose photographs graced the pages of the book I'd just read.

I also remembered that in my dream-state registration in Eckankar, a slim man whose body reflected all the lights of the rainbow had registered me on July 22, 1991; and when my registration material arrived in the mail later, the date I was registered in ECK in the dream state corresponded with the date on the outer registration material.

I concluded that the Mahanta, the Living ECK Master had invited me into Eckankar. Let the Masters of this other path also invite me on the inner planes, like the Mahanta did, if their claim of embodying the original teachings is true!

I Asked the Master to Explain

Another step I took was to ask the spiritual leader of Eckankar to explain to me, if it was necessary, why Paul's *Spiritual Notebook* appeared to copy parts of this older book in certain respects.

Once I had done all this, I concluded to send the book, with a note of thanks, back to the fellow who'd sent it to me. I continued with my ECK practices and never demanded that the Mahanta further explain anything.

Three years elapsed without incident. As a matter of fact, I had completely forgotten the matter. But as it turned out, the Master hadn't forgotten my query.

Get Up There and Read!

I attended an ECK regional seminar in Benin City, Nigeria. I arrived there on Friday, very hungry because I was doing a Friday fast. When I got back to my hotel, I went into contemplation at about half past six for about thirty minutes. It was a prelude to breaking my Friday fast. Incidentally, I find that it's often easier to get out of the body when the body is not loaded with food. And this is what happened.

After I had sung HU for a while, I found myself in the inner worlds in the company of a man I was not able to identify. He led me into a large building. I was unaware at the time that this was one of the many Golden Wisdom Temples described in the ECK teachings. The man led me into a room.

In the room, there was a dais. On the dais stood what I thought was a light box on a framed stand.

"Get up there and read!" the man said in a commanding yet mute language, pointing to the light box.

No Words to Read

I stepped onto the dais and looked at the light box, whose face was in the shape of a heart.

I had expected to see words, but there were none. Only a brilliant light shone out of the heart-shaped face of the light box. Confused, I turned to the man who had commanded me to read.

"There are no words to read!" I complained.

"Read!" he instructed once more.

Perhaps I did not look closely enough, I thought, and I once more pointed my face toward the heart-shaped light box. I looked closely for any faint trace of words or symbols. There were none. Once more, I was about to lift my face from the light box to complain. Then an interesting phenomenon began to take place.

At the Speed of Light

I was reading a book at the speed of light and comprehending the contents perfectly! I quickly turned my full attention to the light box.

The pages of the book I was reading were flipping at a speed an automatic weaving machine would have envied. And yet I was reading them all with perfect comprehension. It didn't take long to realize what book I was reading—*The Spiritual Notebook* by Paul Twitchell! But what I read here was far sweeter than the physical version I had encountered. I eagerly gobbled up the stupendous knowledge that was now pouring into me from this book that contained no words yet was wondrously comprehensible.

"Enough!" my guide's voice broke through.

But on my own I could not lift my face from that

light box. It felt like the pull of a powerful magnet. My companion stepped forward, took me by the shoulder, and led me away from that wonderful light box.

What Was That All About?

"What was that all about?" I asked.

"Suppose you had never read Paul Twitchell's book before," my companion said, "then you had this experience, recorded what you read, and had it published. Would people who knew no better accuse you of copying Paul Twitchell?"

Slowly, the facts dawned on me.

I had been brought face-to-face with the pages of the eternal Shariyat, the inner-plane scripture from which Paul Twitchell and the author of the other book got their respective texts.

The Secret Teachings

Paul Twitchell never claimed he invented the teachings of ECK. Somewhere in these inner worlds, they have always existed, preserved by the ECK Masters, especially those known as the Nine Silent Ones. In *The Shariyat-Ki-Sugmad*, Books One & Two, it says:

> The doctrine of ECK has been handed down to the present age through an unbroken line of ECK Masters who have kept it alive despite whatever suppression has been made against Eckankar.[6]

In his book *The ECK-Vidya, Ancient Science of Prophecy*, Paul Twitchell writes:

> Such secret knowledge as the Egyptian, ancient Greek and eastern religions, and many others became lost. But the ECK wisdom has been kept alive and vital by the Adepts of the Vairagi, deeply hidden in the Temples of Golden Wisdom. This has

been handed down, growing steadily from one generation to the next, ever since the dawn of time in this world. Included in it is the sum total of the ECK-Vidya which these Masters have amassed in the thousands of years in this plane and the others.

Inevitably, all the secrets of the secret wisdom had to be collected in one form, collated, and set down in a permanent form which became the Shariyat-Ki-Sugmad. We find this record of secret wisdom now a holy book divided into approximately twelve books, and each section placed in a Temple of Golden Wisdom in the many planes throughout the universes of God.[7]

For thousands of years, the teachings of ECK had to go underground to survive. Paul Twitchell puts it this way in *The ECK-Vidya, Ancient Science of Prophecy*:

When ECK and Its aspects including the ECK-Vidya became particularly too strong—as in Egypt during the period known as the Third Dynasty 2670–2600 BC, under Djoser, one of the early pharaohs who established the Step Pyramid—it was outlawed and had to go underground.

The priestcraft known as the Amon was responsible for this for they held the political power in Egypt during the ancient times. This was in the era when Gopal Das, one of the early ECK Masters, was then the head of Eckankar here on earth.[8]

Interestingly, just prior to this period, the Kali Yuga, or Iron Age, had begun. Paul Twitchell writes in *The ECK-Vidya*, "This is the age in which we are currently living and was supposedly to have started at midnight between February 17 and 18, 3102 BC."[9] This cycle of cosmic history would see spiritual darkness and intolerance increasingly brood over the affairs of the lower worlds.

The ECK teachings therefore had remained a secret

teaching since the time of Gopal Das in Egypt. Only in 1965, when Paul Twitchell became the Mahanta, the Living ECK Master, did they re-emerge publicly.

In his Wisdom Note in the September 1993 *Mystic World*, Sri Harold Klemp describes Paul Twitchell's main mission thus: "His job was to get the ECK teachings up and running. Time was of no concern."[10]

What I Now Understood

What I understood in contemplation was that, during the period when the ECK teachings lay hidden, the various ECK Masters took people from various religious beliefs (like the Indian guru) into these inner temples. This helped keep the spiritual embers alive till the teachings of the Mahanta could be presented openly to the public again.

This whole experience had been a spiritual test for me. Would I wait for the answers to come in good time, like they did, or would I walk away in a huff with the notion that the teachings of ECK were false?

Talking Dog

In *The Eternal Dreamer*, Mahanta Transcripts, Book 7, Sri Harold Klemp tells a story about how the Mahanta facilitated a conversation, in a dream, between a man and his horse, Sid.[11]

When I read this story, my mind rebelled.

Horses Don't Talk!

I love, trust, and respect the Mahanta, but on this issue, my mind and I went our separate ways.

"No way," said my mind. "Horses don't talk—certainly not to humans!"

I tried to beg and cajole the mind to accept this story. "After all," I said, "the story comes from the Mahanta himself!"

"Hogwash!" The mind spat back.

I was like a parent whose favorite celebrity had walked through his front door but was treated with complete disrespect by his youthful child.

Part of me, like the parent, looked at the Mahanta as a hero who wouldn't lie to me. But the other part, the mind, remained a disrespectful, petulant kid who wouldn't curtsy to royalty. What could I do?

Somehow, a sense of guilt began to creep in. I felt like a parent who had not disciplined his kids properly. Now they were behaving poorly in company.

Chico to the Rescue

Our female dog, Chico, became pregnant. She was also about to come to my rescue, but I had not the slightest idea.

When the time to deliver her litter grew near, I walked her into the garage, carrying a piece of red carpet. Some of my children tagged along for this red-carpet ceremony.

I laid the carpet on the floor and pointed to it.

"This is where you will have your kids in comfort," I said grandly.

Chico sat on her haunches, her large belly looking as if she'd been eating and drinking too much. She gave me that enigmatic dog smile, with crinkled eyes and ears laid back, and of course said absolutely nothing.

"Why didn't Chico respond?" the mind mocked. "Has she not heard of Sid the horse—about humans conversing with animals?"

I left the garage door half open from that day on, in case Chico needed to get in there in a hurry.

Soul Travel

On September 22, 1996, I literally became awake in a dream, a form of Soul Travel.

I stood in the open compound outside my house. On the ground, Chico hovered over her three newborn puppies, which had been delivered in the open air. One puppy was black as night. The second was pure brown, and the third was brown with white markings on its flanks.

Not All Humans Are Stupid

"Didn't you get me, doggy?" I admonished. "I believe I told you there's a red carpet in the garage for you and your kids."

Chico still sat on her haunches, watching me with her liquid eyes.

"Do I have your permission to take these puppies into the garage?" I asked.

There was no response. The enigmatic, Mona Lisa smile persisted.

"Did you not hear me, lady?" I pronounced the words deliberately, as if I were reading from a book. "Do I have your permission . . ."

But I stopped short. Chico *was* speaking to me in a mute language. Her snout was not moving, yet the information was coming through loud and clear. And I heard it in English!

"They'll get in there when they're ready," she said.

The dog smile seemed to broaden when she realized that I had got the message.

"Not all humans are totally stupid," her smile seemed to say. That quickly, I woke up.

Chico's Nowhere to Be Found

The watch by my bed said it was half past four in the morning. I jumped out of bed and went outside. Unfortunately, I had no torch (flashlight).

Chico was nowhere to be found. The first place I looked was inside the garage. My prized red piece of carpet lay neglected on the floor. I noticed a cold draft of air wafting through the garage. This condition of the garage would prove important later on.

I went outside and called out for Chico, to no avail.

Chico had always been a disciplined dog and was never known to abandon her watch duty. Something serious—like pups arriving unannounced—must have happened for Chico to be away from her duty post. I went back in and waited for God's torch to come up in the heavens.

When it was light, I came out with one of my daughters, and we hollered for Chico.

We called and called. Finally my daughter exclaimed, "There's Chico!"

I turned around to where she was pointing. Chico sat on her haunches, the enigmatic smile still plastered on her face. There was a difference in her, though, since I last saw her physically—she was no longer pregnant.

There must be something to my experience, I concluded.

"Where are your pups?" I asked Chico.

She led us to a place that had once been servants' quarters in this rented house. The place was never used by us and lay desolate. It was here that we located the pups.

What Happened

Looking over the evidence, I was able to reconstruct what had happened.

Before she went into parturition, Chico found an old basket. She then picked up some rags and lined the basket with them. No good having your kids start life with pneumonia, eh? After that, she dragged the basket into an empty closet which was free of drafts—unlike that garage where I had placed the red carpet.

When they finally emerged out into the world, Chico picked her pups up one by one and dropped them into the basket. Then, like the dutiful mother she was, she had climbed inside the basket and carefully curled herself around her kids to keep them warm.

I had never had any experience with pups before, so I had no idea that the place I had chosen in the garage was completely inappropriate. But I had meant well, so Chico had not bothered to argue the point when I initially offered that red carpet in the garage.

Clarity of Soul Travel

Looking at the pups, I marveled at the power and clarity of Soul Travel. Just as I had seen before, one pup was black as night, another was brown, and the third brown with patches of white on its flanks.

"Shouldn't we move them to the garage where you put the red carpet?" my daughter asked, breaking my train of thought.

I hesitated before answering. Chico, with her liquid, smiling eyes, watched my face keenly, as if wondering whether I would recall our conversation from earlier that morning. I looked at my daughter, then back to Chico.

"There's at least one human here who, because of Soul Travel, is not *totally* stupid," I assured Chico mutely.

Turning to my daughter, I said, "They'll get in there when they're ready."

Chico beamed so much I thought she might burst into dog applause.

The mind finally gave me a rest from the story of Sid the talking horse. But the mind is the mind. It'd be lost if there were no problem to chew over. The very solution I had just got now sprouted another problem in its place: Who would believe my story about a talking dog?

Space Walk

The project, a hotel that was to have been run by the Sheraton group, had been abandoned twenty years earlier. I had been the supervising architect but not the designer, since it was a turnkey project and the contractors had appointed their own architects for the design.

At first we had insisted that the European contractors submit a complete set of drawings for the consultants and the client government. But the contractors convinced the client that planning, designing, and project execution had to progress simultaneously. Completing the design before starting the project, they said, would make it impossible to keep the target date within the agreed contract period. So the designs would be submitted in stages as the work progressed.

National Karma

One kind of national karma that Nigeria nurses, in my opinion, is the lack of self-esteem. Nigerians, from the top down, believe that anything foreign is superior. A great sportsman or sportswoman might exist within Nigeria, but as long as no foreign country acknowledges the person, Nigerians would never recognize their own.

This karma seems to scatter the focus of the nation, making Nigerians believe that salvation for their national woes will come from foreigners. And this karma was at work in this hotel contract.

I knew quite clearly why the contractors refused to submit a complete set of drawings. They were using this ploy so they could twist the arm of the client, should their contract become threatened for any reason. Take us off this project for any reason whatsoever, they were saying, and you will be left high and dry! Without drawings, how far would you be able to carry the project forward?

But typically, the client agreed with the foreign contractor. I was only a consultant working on behalf of my employer. How could I, the outsider, justifiably weep louder than the bereaved?

Unknown to me, the seed of a positive spiritual lesson hid behind this event, and I would see it sprout twenty years down the road.

Coup

One and a half years into the project, a military coup took place.

The incoming military government, in typical fashion, demonized and suspended all ongoing programs of the government they had taken over.

Once the new government failed to honor the contract, the contractors demobilized from the site. Neither the client nor the consultant—that's me—had a complete set of drawings of the project.

I traveled to Europe to ask the contractors to release the drawings to us, since the client had already paid for them. But the contractors demanded a punitive payment of three and a half million US dollars before they would release the drawings. The original charge for the drawings was about a million US dollars, which had already been settled. Of course the client refused to deal. The bottom line was that the client thus did not have the drawings for the project as it stood, and it had to be abandoned.

Reappointed

Twenty years after the project had been abandoned, the same consultant—that's me—was reappointed to continue with it. There was still no shred of a drawing in our possession to restart this multimillion-dollar project. As a matter of fact, the project came to me because of the lack of drawings. And now the client was making impossible demands, such as getting a design history of the project together in only two months!

Surveying and redrawing this complex building would ordinarily take the better part of a year. I took some preliminary steps to find a way around the problem, but they proved futile. Then I became a bit scared.

Was this brief feasible, or should we drop it?

Walk Over Empty Space?

I got my answer in the dream state.

I am at the project site. As I stand at the main entrance, preparing to walk into the building, I discover that the floor is not there! How am I going to even walk into the building to do the initial survey when the floor is nothing but empty space?

"U ndyar u pel!" the Mahanta says in a voice from the ethers. It's a saying in my native tongue. Roughly translated, it means "If you dare put a foot forward, you will cross over!"

Step into empty space?

But the Mahanta has spoken. Besides, there is no other way in.

I stand at the lip of the gaping chasm where the floor should be. I take a deep breath and put a foot forward, stepping into the abyss.

I find myself simultaneously in the Soul body, as if from a distance.

Every time I put a foot forward, a square concrete block sprouts up in the empty space to receive the foot. As soon as the foot is removed, the block seemingly evaporates!

I am halfway across when I begin to laugh. Then I wake up.

Now awake, I wondered how I would put into practice my dream of "stepping into empty space" in this project.

Inside the Belly

While I thought about that, I had another dream.

I see someone passing. The Master's voice speaks from the ethers:

"He has those Sheraton drawings inside his belly!"

I wonder about this. Should I now grab this fellow to get access to those drawings?

In the next instant, I find myself sitting opposite this fellow who has the project drawings in his belly.

After a while, I notice that a flexible pipe, a hundred millimeters (four inches) in diameter, now connects this fellow and me by our bellies! From the ethers, the voice of the Mahanta gives a command to the other fellow:

"OK, transmit!"

At this instant, the contents of this man's belly begin to flow into me.

In contemplation, the phrase *gut feeling* occurred to me. I knew that this was one way I could get at those drawings.

I went into town and began to scout around, using my gut feeling to fish out all those people who had been directly or remotely connected with this project.

The first and most useful person I found in my search had been a language interpreter on the project. He went around with me to locate some of the artisans—masons, electricians, plumbers, and so forth—who had worked on various aspects of the project. Many were out of work and comforting themselves at drinking joints.

Tattered Blueprints

As I interviewed these people, odd sheets of tattered blueprints—drawings for the part of the project each individual was involved with—would surface here and there—for the right price.

A painter, who had become a personal friend of one of the European contractors, had a complete set of architectural drawings in small scale. He had been given this set to make a bid for the painting job. These drawings sold for the highest price—fifty thousand naira.

Since the drawings I got were mostly tattered blueprints, I set up a special studio in my office and employed four top draftsmen. From this ragtag information, we began to reconstruct the design history of the project on tracing paper. We could then make as many blueprints as required by the client. Very soon, I had the full reconstruction of the most vital design aspects. But one important drawing was missing—the kitchen.

The kitchen for this project was actually to be three kitchens in one—French, Chinese, and an all-purpose kitchen.

Among the drawings I had recovered so far, there was no shred of information on the kitchen, and that presented the worst technical difficulty. The space allocated for the kitchen had openings of various sizes and shapes in both the roof and floor to accommodate all kinds of service pipes, wires, and exhaust pipes. There was no way to sort one hole from another.

More Inner Help

Once more, I went into contemplation and asked the Master for help. And again I got an answer in a dream.

I am bathing in a river with other people. Someone fishes out a perfect set of some of the hotel drawings and brings them to me.

Two days later, a man walked into my office with a large brown envelope.

"I learnt you are in the market for Sheraton drawings," he said. "Do these interest you?"

When he pulled the blueprints from the envelope and unfolded them, I had to make a great effort to hide my extreme excitement. If he had seen how I felt, he might have doubled or even tripled his asking price.

This stranger placed before me the most perfectly preserved blueprints of all I had seen and bought so far. And they were the kitchen drawings with full details!

Looking at them, I knew there was no way we could have reconstructed these drawings from memory or done without them. The details to consider—matching up all those small openings in the floor and roof with their specified functions—were stupendous. And because I had the presence of mind to keep an indifferent facial expression, the price was also right.

When I finally presented the complete design history of the project to the client within the given time frame, even the architects in the Works Ministry marveled at the feat.

They never would have believed it if I'd said research through the dream state had helped me reconstruct these lost drawings.

Spiritual Virus

Nine years before a certain former high initiate would leave the path of ECK, the Inner Master was on hand to warn me of the impending rebellion and to show me what I could do to protect myself from the fallout. But for a long time, I was unaware of what this warning was about.

In time, I would discover there is only one option for a true chela of the Mahanta during a spiritual crisis of this nature—to simply continue steadily on the path to spiritual freedom that the Mahanta has mapped out. Stopping even briefly to watch a fight that fallen angels wage against the ECK can have seriously messy consequences—like a computer virus!

A Warning Dream

Here is the warning dream I had, nine years ahead of time.

I am going to an Eckankar seminar. The seminar venue is said to be "beyond Lagos."

For some unexplained reason, I find myself in Lagos, in the hotel suite of the Mahanta, the Living ECK Master. I am stunned.

"I never expected this privilege," I stammer.

The Master's face shows concern, and he leans forward, listening intently to my overwhelmed stutter. I notice that he is looking ruddy and healthy. He sits in front of a very large picture window, with the ocean behind him. I sit facing him.

In the mute language of the inner worlds, he orders room service. When the food is brought, I discover that it has been served inside mussel shells (my dream symbol for the secret teachings). *The food is a tangy-tasting mix of fresh green vegetables.* (The strong taste of the food promises a strong teaching experience. Green, the color of the physical plane, symbolizes that this lesson will one day become physical reality.)

As we eat, the Master tells me a story. He speaks in the same mute language as before, but I can hear him very clearly. Very soon, the words turn into pictures and the pictures into a movie, which in turn solidifies into real scenes.

Boat Full of Crabs

A boat full of crabs floats on the ocean. There is the usual scuffling and pinching one would expect in a boat overcrowded with crabs. At one point, one crab has had enough. He wants out. He tries to get back into the ocean that offers the limitless freedom this cramped boat couldn't. This crab seems to recall that the ocean had been his original home anyway.

However, as he makes his way up to the edge of the boat to get out, another crab reaches out and grabs the escaping crab in its claws. The first crab does not know what to make of this unprovoked aggression. His only aim has been to get out into freedom—not into a fight.

At this point, Sri Harold takes a pinch of his food and then continues.

Not knowing what to do, the crab that wants out surrenders the situation to the God of the crabs. Once he does this, another crab, more aggressive than the assailant, reaches out from inside the boat and grabs the attacker in its vicious claws. The assailant can't believe this. He is not like the nonresponsive crab he attacked. Abandoning his victim, who never once responded to his attack, he turns his full attention on his assailant to teach him a lesson.

In the scuffle that ensues, both fighters fall into the very bottom of the crowded boat. A free-for-all naturally breaks out in these crowded conditions.

The Master's eyes shine as he warms to his story.

"Now the escaping crab has three options open to him," he says. *"For one, he can jump back down into the boat and join the fight if he so chooses. His second option is to sit and watch the goings-on. But,"* the Master concludes, *"let's not forget his initial purpose—to get back into the ocean. The fight below has given him a better opportunity than ever to advance to his initial goal!"*

I recorded that dream experience on Saturday, December 17, 1994. It took nine years for that story to manifest in my life. When it did, I would see that the dream had been a warning.

Web Browsing

I traveled one week early to the 2003 ECK Worldwide Seminar in the United States of America. It would turn out to be that "seminar beyond Lagos."

When I arrived in Newark, New Jersey, I stayed at a friend's house, waiting for the seminar days to arrive. Then my friend and I would fly to the seminar locale, Minneapolis.

My friend and his wife worked long hours. Most of the time, I was left at home alone, and I passed the time browsing the Internet. This Web browsing would kick-start the crab story.

While trying to access the Eckankar Web site, I came upon the Web site of a former high initiate who had recently left Eckankar and was challenging the ECK teachings. Included was an open letter to the Mahanta, the Living ECK Master, inviting a response to the challenge. The letter, and any response, would supposedly allow ECKists to test their loyalties to ECK as they wished.

Crab Story Playing Out

I was taken aback.

This former high initiate had been sent several times

to speak at ECK seminars in our country. I was very disappointed. However, I read the Web site to the end. I might have gone back to it again and again without the slightest idea that my continued interest in the site was part of the crab story playing out. Instead of heading out of the boat, I was sitting at the edge of the boat watching the goings-on below. There were consequences!

When this whole episode was over, I discovered what was really happening here was that this person was attacking the link various students had with the Mahanta. In other words, the supposed attack on the ECK teachings was actually an attack on the spiritual journey of each ECK chela—including me—an attempt to prevent us from getting out of the crowded boat, back into the ocean of spiritual freedom.

One of the ploys this crab employed was to look for a fight—get the Living ECK Master to respond. That would bring the Master down to his level. But unfortunately for this crab, he was not getting the fight he wanted. The Master kept mum and let the others decide for themselves what this attack was worth. The frustration of the attacker was quite obvious when I read his next letter of challenge to the Mahanta.

Another Aggressive Crab

In his second challenge, it became obvious that the attacking crab had now himself come under "unprovoked" attack by someone outside of Eckankar. He threatened this person with a crippling lawsuit.

The fight in the boat was heating up!

But because I had not yet recognized what was going on as a playing out of that nine-year-old crab story, I also forgot a very important aspect of my part in the unfolding saga.

Choices

I read that Web site over and over, even after I was back in Nigeria. And that was tantamount to sitting halfway out of the boat, watching the fight instead of continuing with my climb to freedom!

Pretty soon, I discovered the images and impressions of that fight had seeped into my consciousness like a computer virus. An invisible group now hung around at the dark fringes of my consciousness every time I tried to go into contemplation. This faceless group began to mock my beliefs, my efforts at the spiritual exercises, and even my trust in the Mahanta. Going into contemplation became like walking into a war zone—which is just what it was, since a psychic war was raging. And the pawns in that game were ECK students like me!

"What good are those spiritual exercises?" these hangers-on jeered every time I tried to go into contemplation. "You really believe what the so-called Mahanta is dishing out to deceive all those fools out there?"

This went on for just over a month before I caught on to what was happening. Once the malady was out in the open, I knew that I needed a doctor to get rid of these unwanted guests. So I turned to the Mahanta—my spiritual doctor.

I Ask Wah Z for Help

My first action was to write an initiate report to the Mahanta, asking for help in moving this lot along. The next action was to do a spiritual exercise. An inner nudge came to me that this lot were slowly poisoning my mind from their hiding place in the lower Astral Plane, to which they had gravitated.

I did a spiritual exercise using the word *Kala*, a charged word for the Astral Plane. As soon as I started the spiritual exercise, a rooster, in all its proud plumes and finery, strutted before my Spiritual Eye.

This must be the chief of these viruses, I thought. It was plain to see that pride and attachment had tripped this former high initiate and his followers, now operating on the lower Astral Plane.

I invited Wah Z, the Mahanta, into my space. When he arrived, I listed all those distractions brought into my space; I wrote them down on a piece of paper and handed it over to Wah Z. I requested that he get the unwanted guests out of my space.

Just that fast, the mechanical efforts I had been making for over a month to do the spiritual exercises gave way to immediate success. In fact, the dissolution of the problem was so complete, I now was having difficulty pulling out of the spiritual exercise. This was a complete contrast to what had been happening recently.

When I came out of contemplation, I wondered why I had not thought of this approach earlier. Paradoxically, I also knew the answer to my own question.

Where Light Meets Darkness

When one is absorbed in watching something as negative as a psychic battle, one has little time for constructive thinking. Very soon, what the eyes see and the ears hear ends up poisoning the emotions, which eventually poison the mind. This gradually leads one in consciousness to the fringes where light meets darkness—where the dark forces always lurk.

Even those who don't take sides but just sit and watch these goings on are soon swayed by the emotions caused by what the eyes see and the ears hear. Now poisoned, undecided people begin to wonder about where truth really resides. The presence of the Light and Sound of God in the person's life begins to dim. Eventually, a more careless watcher can become so weak or confused or both that he falls back to the bottom of the boat. Once there, he finds only one option open to him—joining the fight. His spiritual goal of getting back into the Ocean of Love and Mercy becomes a dim memory.

The Mahanta Is Always Here

I was fortunate indeed that I had had fair warning nine years earlier, and even more fortunate that the Master helped me catch on to what was happening before it was too late.

The Mahanta, I discovered, is always here during these tests, helping us decide what's best for us spiritually. The spiritual exercises and other ECK practices provide the link to him.

Try this spiritual exercise today!

— ⌒ —

Formula Four Technique

Formula Four is for visiting the Mental Plane, which is the source of philosophy, ethics, moral teachings, and aesthetics.

Before you begin, write in your dream journal that you are using this technique.

Chant HU four times, then breathe four times. Keep doing this for fifteen to twenty minutes, before bed or in contemplation. Lightly keep in mind that you want to visit the Mental Plane.

Take note of your dreams and record them in the morning.

—Adapted from "The Formula Technique"
in *The Spiritual Exercises of ECK*
by Harold Klemp[12]

7

Subconscious Spam

Then comes the Etheric Plane, which is the unconscious, or subconscious, area. It is the high part of the mind that houses unconscious attitudes, some of which were acquired through karmic experiences in past lives. This often accounts for why we have certain talents or why we are instinctively drawn to one person and repelled by another.

—Harold Klemp,
The Art of Spiritual Dreaming[1]

When I was chairman of the local-government council, I was invited to be interviewed live on the state radio-station program *Personality of the Week*.

Live Broadcast

My interviewer was a born-again Christian. As the interview progressed, he asked me about my philosophy of life. Of course, my philosophy of life was the ECK way of life. I never quoted any holy scriptures and never mentioned the name of any religion. All I spoke about came from examples from life—things so self-evident

155

that there was really nothing about them to challenge.

This obviously worried my interviewer. He must have been wondering *Is he with us or against us?*

Of course I was not against anybody at all. I was with the currents of life itself! And life provides room for the Christian, Muslim, ECKist, or even the atheist. Apparently, this man was not so generous.

Life, to him, was compartmentalized into different religions. As far as he was concerned, it was just like politics. He wanted to know where you stood with him. And I had not made a stand at all during my interview. He therefore decided to smoke me out to see with whom I was running—the foxes or the hares.

"Are you a Christian?" he asked me out of the blue.

Are You a Christian?

If this fellow had decided to inquire in a noncombative way, he would have asked me, What's your religion?

My answer, if it were not clear enough, would have then elicited further discussion. The listening public would have had a chance to judge me from a fairer perspective.

But this was a "Christian" state.

In Nigeria, many who are not Muslims—apart from ECKists—call themselves Christians for convenience. And Christians are comfortable with that. Even if you are not a practicing Christian, if you just say that you are one, there shall be peace for you. In some states in Nigeria, to dare say you are not a Christian, when you are not a Muslim, is considered an act of aggression against Christianity! Such a person is considered a pagan—a derogatory term Nigerians inherited from the retreating British colonialists and have never relinquished.

Being a Muslim would have been more forgivable.

But everyone knew I wasn't. Saying I was a Christian, even when no one ever saw me in a Christian church lately, would have been acceptable. But to say No, I am not a Christian? The ears of most of my listeners would have filled with wax. No one would have been prepared to listen to the rest of what I had to say.

Who wanted a pagan for a political hero? Some had heard of Eckankar, but many thought Eckankar was a fringe Christian sect.

Boxed into a Corner

Both of us knew that I was boxed into a corner. And it suited my interviewer just fine.

I apparently had two choices open to me: tell a lie or ruin my interview. I was between the proverbial devil and the deep blue sea. I knew that I needed one of those inner nudges from the Mahanta to escape.

To buy time and see what would pop up from within, I asked my interviewer, "What is a Christian?"

He was prepared for that one. I wouldn't weasel my way out of the corner so easily.

"You are the personality being interviewed," he said. "Our listeners are not interested in what I think or say. It's you they're listening to," he said, still leaving me firmly in that tight corner. His smile did not reach his eyes.

During his short response, I sang HU and asked the Mahanta for help.

I asked another question: "If you winnowed cultural trappings and politics out of religions, say Christianity and Islam, and got to the grain of the teachings of these two religions concerning love and service, would you see any real fundamental differences in the goals of the two faiths?"

This time, he was more generous. "No, I guess not."

That Golden Thread

Just that quick, the inner nudge popped into my consciousness.

"OK," I said, "I am that!"

"I beg your pardon?"

"My religion is that golden thread, beyond the reach of politics and culture, that unites both Christianity and Islam," I said.

He gave a short bark, which he must have hoped would pass for a show of mirth. It did not reach his eyes, and I understood. I had just miraculously slipped out of the tight corner he had boxed me into, and he was not too happy about that. But that was now his problem, not mine.

From there till the interview ended, he didn't ask any more awkward questions.

"Whew! That was close," I said inwardly to the Mahanta. Thanks to his timely inner guidance, I left the studio without having told a lie or offended my audience.

Since that interview, now and then someone will come to me and ask, "What's that golden thread that links Christianity and Islam?"

Away from the microphone of the broadcasting station, I can look at the inquirer and decide more leisurely what the questioner wants or can take. Then I give it as best I can—just enough and no more.

Missing Pages

It was the closing day of the September 2001 ECK regional seminar in Lagos. I had a strong urge to buy a copy of *The Days of Soul Journal*, a dream journal in calendar format published by Eckankar.

For each day and at the beginning of each month, the journal features a special quote from the Mahanta, the Living ECK Master for the student's contemplation.

I was short of money, but I borrowed from a friend. The journal came sealed in cellophane, so I decided to open it only when I got home. Back home, I got a surprise.

Nineteen calendar pages were missing from this journal! To compound the mystery, the missing pages were not scattered around the book but were consecutive, starting at August 14 and ending on September 1.

My first thought was that it might have been a printing error common to the whole run of journals. But when I compared my copy of the dream journal with those that others had purchased, it turned out all the other books had all their pages.

At first I decided that, at the earliest opportunity, I would return this journal for a replacement.

But certain elements in this "mistake" made me begin to think that this must be a special journal!

First, I began to look at the prodigious odds of this mistake happening at all, and then the chances of this particular volume coming to me.

Special Message

The odds of this high-quality publication passing through quality control with nineteen calendar pages missing were hard to calculate.

Eckankar is also a worldwide religion. That volume could have been shipped to any of a hundred or so countries where the ECK community exists. Yet, it came to Nigeria. At this seminar, many ECKists must have bought this new book. But when I came to the bookroom counter and asked for *The Days of Soul Journal*, a disinterested volunteer reached out and pulled this particular sealed volume with nineteen calendar pages missing from it and gave it to me.

My conclusion? The ECK had a special message for me. Now it was time to decipher it!

The first missing page, August 14, coincided with the expiry date of my yearly registration in Eckankar.

Another coincidence that breathed more mystery into this remarkable journal was the number of missing calendar pages—nineteen. I had earlier had a number of dreams where I was given a key to a hotel room—number 19.

I wondered: Would something happen to me, causing me to pass out for nineteen days? Or would I be in deep trouble, without hope of escape, for nineteen days?

It was also quite interesting to read the quotes just before and after the missing pages. The two complemented each other as if no pages had gone missing between them.

Becoming Aware of God's Love

Quote for August 13:

> This love [God's] is everywhere: in a child's hug, in a puppy's eagerness to play, and in the blooming of wildflowers on the lawn. The more we can accept divine love, the more we can receive. Yet, accepting God's love is only half of it. The other part is giving it back through service.
>
> *Wisdom of the Heart*, Book 1[2]

Quote for September 2:

> You, as an individual, are to become more aware of God's love. What makes you aware of this love?
>
> The experiences you have in your daily life.
>
> And the experiences that teach you about love are often those of pain. Pain teaches God's love. We don't like pain, we don't like change, but they are

blessings in disguise. They teach us to become more godlike.

What Is Spiritual Freedom?
Mahanta Transcripts, Book 11[3]

I alternately thrill and tremble every time I read and contemplate these quotes, particularly when August 14 approaches each year. Because, honestly, I am still deciphering the message! It's like the promise of a rose. The flower smells nice, yet it comes on a branch with stinging thorns. But whatever form it takes, I'm sure it will be a blessing in disguise.

Turbulent Flight

Sometime later I had the following dream, which I call the Legislator's Flight Problem dream.

I am part of a group of legislators scheduled to fly over the Atlantic. Prior to departure, I dream the plane is going to plunge into the ocean and everyone on board is going to die! Now, I have to decide: Should I trust in God and make the trip, or should I assume God has warned me via the dream and forgo the flight? I decide to dare fate.

As I thought about the dream, I was able to crack the dream symbol for the word *legislator*. I discovered that in this particular dream it symbolized the Third Initiate.

In April 2003, I had been a Third Initiate in Eckankar for about three years, and I decided to travel to the first ECK Spiritual Skills Seminar, in Washington, DC. Unknown to me, this decision would turn out to be the Legislator's Flight Problem dream trip!

During this trip, I would be in training to face the fear of death, because shortly after my return I would face a sudden major operation. By then, my flight problems would have helped me develop more trust in the Mahanta.

Random Computer Check

My flight to Washington, DC, started innocuously enough. We got to Newark Liberty International Airport without even any turbulence. It was the short connecting flight to Washington Dulles that started it all.

"Our plane has been selected at random for a computer check," the captain told us as we started to taxi to the runway. "These checks are quite routine," he assured us.

Ours ended up anything but routine.

Our plane, selected at random for these "routine checks," failed to pass the computer check. In fact it had a major fault which could not be repaired immediately.

"We'll get you a new plane," the ground crew said.

The new plane took four hours to show up. But when we finally arrived at Washington Dulles without incident, I put the matter out of my head. It was just one of those things.

Volunteer

During the ECK Spiritual Skills Seminar, I volunteered to help.

"What area would you want to assist in?" the volunteer organizer asked me.

"Anyplace where there is a need," I offered.

Inside, I said something different: *Anyplace but the children's room!* With ten kids, I have had my full share of parenting.

"We would be grateful if you could help in the children's room with registration," the lady in charge at the volunteers desk said.

Ouch! I said inside. But outwardly, I put up a brave face, as if working in the children's room would be the greatest pleasure.

I had no idea, but an event that would prove critical to my survival—and my fellow passengers on the return flight—was awaiting me at the children's registration desk.

I had registered the children and was sitting there waiting for their program to end and their parents to come for them, when a team of ebullient young adults entered the room. Styled the "ECK Press," these four ECKists with a movie camera and klieg lights surrounded my desk before I was sure where they were heading.

"ECK Press" Interview

"Could we interview you for an ECK program that may be aired later—somewhere, somehow?" they asked me.

Always ready to help with the Mahanta's mission, I responded, "Sure!" They had me sign a release form, then the interview started.

"What have you gained at this seminar?" they asked.

"I came here with a number of objectives in mind," I said, looking into the camera. "One was to find ways to help set up an ECK center in my place back home, and another was to improve my skill as an ECK writer. I am surer of my direction in life now; I now know where I am going spiritually."

They nodded vigorously at that. Then the next question came.

"How did you meet the Mahanta?"

It was my favorite subject.

I began to dig into the Lagos-weekend experience—the one I related at the beginning of this book. I had hardly gone halfway into the story, when the youth holding the camera put his ear to the machine and took on a quizzical look.

"Hold it! Hold it!" he said to the person asking the

question. "There's something going on inside this camera!"

The klieg lights were switched off, and the young man holding the camera opened the battery chamber.

Pretty Hot Stuff

"My oh my!" he exclaimed. "Never seen this in all my life!"

It turned out that the dry-cell batteries, advertised as leakproof, had burst!

"Man," he said in his American twang, looking at me with respect in his eyes. "What you are saying must be pretty hot stuff for this to happen!"

He slotted fresh batteries into the camera, and the interview proceeded to its end.

This event left one impression on me—the first-time meeting of the chela and the Mahanta packs a spiritual punch. Even inanimate dry-cell batteries, upon hearing the story, may weep tears of joy!

I had no idea that in a few days' time, I would need to recall this event from the subconscious to save my skin and perhaps that of others.

Return Flight

After the seminar, I took the return flight home. The journey from Minneapolis to Amsterdam to Kano was without incident. But it looked like whatever was pulling the bad strings on these flights particularly had it in for the local legs of the journey. According to my dream premonition, we were supposed to crash into the ocean, not dry land. But who is to say just how dream symbols will play out?

The KLM plane that had taken us to Kano was now taxiing to takeoff for the short hop to Abuja, when we got an ominous announcement such as we had heard at Newark.

"There's a slight problem in the cargo hold of this plane," the captain announced. "Won't take long to fix," he said.

He was wrong about the second part.

"The problem is a little more complicated than we had envisaged," the captain announced, swallowing his first words. "It'll take a while to fix."

It took about an hour before we were airborne for the forty-five-minute flight to Abuja, my final destination.

But we were not yet out of the woods.

Flashes of Lightning

I had closed my eyes to relax. When I opened them again, I saw strange flashes lighting the sky in the direction of Abuja. A storm on the horizon? When you are up there in the sky, and particularly when you are coming in to land, the last thing you want to see is a violent storm brewing. But that is exactly what was going on.

Three times the pilot tried to bulldoze through the storm to land, and three times he aborted. He had to, if he wanted to keep the plane in one piece!

At each approach, people screamed as the wind whipped the aircraft around like a small toy. God and different saviors got mentioned aloud time and time again. For almost two hours, it was as if God was looking for some Jonah (me?) to throw out of this plane before the storm would calm enough for a safe landing.

All Kinds of Spiritual Exercises

All the time this was going on, I was trying all kinds of spiritual exercises. But none that I tried let me strongly feel the presence of the Mahanta in the plane. It was most strange. Why was I unable to open myself to the Mahanta in this situation?

I started wondering if the "legislator" might take the plunge after all. Then my interview at the ECK Spiritual Skills Seminar in Washington, DC, wafted into my consciousness: "How did you first meet the Mahanta?" The impression breathed softly into my consciousness.

I began to reconstruct that first conscious inner meeting with the Mahanta in Lagos, which finally led me into Eckankar. I got so deep into it that I forgot I was inside a plane that had been having trouble touching ground for almost two hours.

At the height of the exercise, the Mahanta once more drifted out of the sky in his starry body, sitting in the lotus position just as I had seen him in the Lagos experience. Immediately, the voice of the captain brought me out of the contemplation.

"Ladies and gentlemen, we will be landing at Nnamdi Azikiwe International Airport, Abuja, in a few minutes' time!"

Eye of the Storm

After we landed, the pilot explained things.

The storm had taken Abuja in its grip for over two hours, its eye sitting directly over the airport for that long. The pilot had wanted to return to Kano but was afraid that the storm would chase him and arrive ahead of us.

Then, just as sudden as it had been persistent, the eye of the storm had shifted north, allowing us to land.

The "legislator" thus ended his flight over the ocean without plunging into either it or the hard ground. But the experience had helped me develop more trust in

God, and I was much more ready for the prostatectomy that awaited me a few weeks after landing.

If you are an ECKist in trouble, and nothing else seems to work, perhaps you can try recalling how you first encountered the Mahanta in this life. The event packs a spiritual punch.

Major Surgery

Back in June 1996, I began to have dreams of coming physical problems. It was a disquieting time for me since my money situation was not good. Later, I would discover that the money problem was also a mask behind which my fears lurked—the possibility of confirming serious ill health from a doctor frightened me. Without money, I had a good excuse not to go poking around in my body. I let sleeping dogs lie.

Dream-State Prostatectomy

Seven years before it happened, I had a prostatectomy—the removal of an enlarged prostate—in the dream state. When I reported these dreams and early signs to our family doctor, also an ECKist, he waved it aside.

"That kind of problem is for very old people," he said dismissively. "You are certainly not yet in that age bracket!"

I liked to believe him, for a number of reasons.

For one, I was afraid of an operation—pure and simple. Even taking an injection was an ordeal for me. An operation was a medical trip to the moon, as far as I was concerned. My doctor's dismissive comment became my straw to grasp at. I should have insisted on an examination, but I didn't.

"The problem is not there," I told myself, even though,

as the years rolled by, passing water was becoming more and more an ordeal.

The second reason was money—or rather the lack of it. We had fallen on hard times. Without money, I hoped the ECK might provide an easy way out—an inner healing that would let me dodge the dreaded surgery.

I was wrong. So was my doctor.

Since the last quarter of the year 2000, while my ability to pass water dwindled, my finances went in the other direction. They improved dramatically, thus removing one of the crutches I clung to in order to avoid the medical examination.

I Couldn't Run Anymore

One day, I visited the National Hospital in Abuja and casually mentioned my problem to a surgeon whom a friend had introduced to me.

The National Hospital, Abuja, is one of the better health facilities in the country. I had money, yet I kept dodging, citing a busy schedule, when the doctor advised that I make an appointment.

Perhaps the doctor noticed this, because one day I took a friend to him for a problem. He had hardly finished examining the patient, when he turned to me.

"Let's look at your matter now," he said.

I couldn't run anymore.

When I returned from the 2003 ECK Spiritual Skills Seminar in Washington, DC, I was scheduled to conclude the tests and examination. Then things began to move rather fast.

After I had scans, X-rays, and ECGs, several needles were stuck in me to draw blood for one sample and then another. Finally the result came: I had an enlarged prostate. I was passing only fifty percent of the urine in my bladder at each session.

The doctors wanted to know if other organs in the body had been affected by this urine retention, so several more tests were carried out. To my relief, they showed no organ damage. And the ECG had indicated that my heart was also in excellent shape. To me, this was the first medical confirmation of the healing I got from Paul Twitchell a few years back.

The PSA test, which would have suggested a possible malignancy, came up negative too.

"The PSA test is not conclusive," the doctor said. "It is only when we do the tissue test on the organ, when it is removed, that we can be certain."

That bit did not worry me at all. Somehow, I had this inner assurance that I had no cancer.

Once all the tests were in, I was given a short three days' notice for the operation. Perhaps the doctors feared that I might abscond.

But while this process went on, I discovered that I had developed a surprising degree of detachment to the whole situation. I believe that the return flight to Abuja after the ECK seminar had something to do with this newfound detachment and confidence.

I drove the three and a half hours home from Abuja to inform my wife, who was to accompany me to the hospital. Apart from my closest friend, we kept it a secret. We did not need public speculations about my health.

Hospital Ward

The days before the operation passed in a blur. I had booked the most reasonably priced bed space in the hospital—a ward containing six beds, three on each side of the room.

On my left was an orthopedic case, a military ex-serviceman who got entangled with a hit-and-run driver. On my right was a cancer patient. On the other side of the room was a fellow with a melanoma, some kind of vicious skin cancer. Next to him was a fellow who had suffered an accident and had been taken to a cheap health facility prior to coming here. The bed-sores he developed had turned gangrenous and were now more life-threatening than his original problem. Last on the list was a pastor with high blood pressure, diabetes, and urinary incontinence. He came from the same locale as I. After I was shown my bed space, I went over to greet him, and he asked me when I was going to bring the patient for whom I had secured the bed space.

"I am the patient!" I told him. The pastor's eyes widened in surprise. "You, the patient?" he said, looking at my apparently healthy physique. "There is no telling these days," he said. "We might look green like a healthy fruit outside, but who knows what worms are eating us from inside?"

Prayer Vultures

In the few days before and after the operation, I observed how people in these wards, full of fear as they hover over the thin line that separates life from death, become pawns in the hands of prayer vultures. At first I wondered why some of my fellow patients would allow several prayer groups or individuals to pray over them again and again. But it soon dawned on me why.

People who lean on faith as the final arbiter of truth often find themselves in the position of a gambler. If it was not God that gave them this illness, it must be the other fellow. Now, as they hover at the borders of death, they are trying hard to get God to become aware that that bad fellow had got through to them. Would this prayer warrior get the ear of God? Unsure, they shop around.

As an ECKist, I knew that my problems lay with the Mahanta and me. Finis! I had a problem because of what I did in the past. Now the Mahanta would help me find the best route through this problem. Why would I need a prayer warrior?

I could only feel compassion for my ward mates who were furiously shopping around for the right prayers to save themselves from death. But I would have given a gold medal to one lady for her heroic attempt to pray over me.

Can We Share the Word of God?

She was heavy with child, but that did not dampen her ardor at all. After praying over four other patients in the room, it was apparently not enough for her.

"Can we share the word of God together?" she requested, approaching my bed with a smile.

"Are you sure we have the same word of God?" I asked.

"Where do you go to church?"

"Eckankar," I said.

"Yeah, I've been watching them on the Abuja TV channels on Sundays."

She might have watched, but apparently she never listened. She thought Eckankar was a no-good fringe Christian sect.

"We are not Christians," I said.

"At least you believe in the word of God?" she said, holding up a large, floppy Bible.

I had a copy of the combined volume of *The Shariyat-Ki-Sugmad*, and I held it up for her to examine. "This is our bible," I said.

Either out of fear or because she thought it was inconsequential, she refused to touch *The Shariyat* or even give it a proper look.

"Surely, Jesus features in your teachings," she said hopefully. I held up the picture of the Mahanta by my bedside. "This is our Jesus," I declared.

Her eyes screamed "Blasphemy!" but she wanted to convert me. After all, this might turn out to be my last chance to be saved from the heat of hell. So, instead of exclaiming, she just shrugged and went on.

"Is there nothing I can do for you?" she asked.

"At least we can smile at each other," I said.

The Bible doesn't say anything about saving souls through smiles, so she was not consoled even when I beamed my best in her direction. Not knowing what to do next, she threw her Christian blessings at me in the hope that they might do some good, somehow.

"I bless and cover you in the blood of Jesus," she said.

Perhaps she expected me to say amen. Instead, I once more bared my fangs in the best possible smile I could muster and waved as she walked out of the room. Someone who had tried that hard deserved no less. To a fisherman, the one that got away always looks like the fattest fish, and she had my sympathy.

Positive End

A positive end, as far as I was concerned, came of her efforts.

A few minutes after she left the room, someone entered in a wheelchair.

"I am an ECKist in the next ward," said the man, a motor-accident victim. "A pregnant woman came to pray over me. When I told her why I couldn't accept her prayers, she told me, 'There's another one of your type in the next room!'"

We embraced, sang HU together, and thanked the Mahanta for turning that lady's unsolicited efforts to some good.

Entity

The prayer vultures were not the only unsolicited visitors I had while recuperating in the hospital.

I had all kinds of tubes running into and out of my body after the operation. I could not move and was in a weakened state. Somehow, a female entity from the lower Astral Plane—someone I may have dallied with in the past—saw my condition as an opportunity for a reengagement. She jumped out of the marshes and made a beeline for me.

"I am looking for my lost boyfriend," she declared.

I may have been immobilized in the physical, but not in the inner worlds. Not with all those lessons in Soul Travel.

I jumped out of my immobilized body and went into a crouch.

"Come on," I beckoned like the famous wrestler The Rock, "let's get it on!"

She looked in my eyes and then at my crouch. She saw a fight, not lust. That was not what she'd been after. Just that quickly, she jumped back into the marshes from where she'd come.

I almost laughed out loud. If only those who had come to frighten me with their prayers could have seen me now!

The freedom a spiritual student experiences in the company of the Mahanta, the Living ECK Master can never be imagined by those outside ECK!

Rest in Peace?

About the fourth day after the operation, an ECK Master with Afghan features called me out into a meadow in brassy sunlight.

"Get ready for training in certain aspects of Soul Travel," he said.

Unbelievable!

My physical body was trussed up like a chicken ready for the barbecue. I turned and looked at a group of people lazing about under a shade tree. When was it time for me to rest?

He read my thoughts.

"Those whom the Mahanta has chosen as his own never rest—under any conditions!" he said.

It occurred to me that some who did not make it out of this hospital, and were not ECKists, would have "Rest in Peace" on the caskets that bore their remains to the grave—as if resting in peace was such a hot idea. If it were, there would be more volunteers! Few go to this "peaceful rest" without a fight.

As a follower of the Mahanta, I confirmed there is no rest for me—in injury or even death. Maybe that's one reason I don't fear dying. I know I won't be stuck resting till Judgment Day—whenever that might be!

I am grateful to the Mahanta for these lessons!

Oh—and I got out of the hospital alive and cancer-free.

Try this spiritual exercise today!

Baju

There are many spiritual words one can try out in contemplation. The word *Baju* (BAH-joo) is especially for the Etheric Plane, one of the heavens beyond the physical realm.

The Shariyat-Ki-Sugmad, Books One & Two, says: "The top of the Mental Plane, the Etheric Plane, is known as the unconscious, because it is a clearer channel for those seeking to become the instrument of God. Psychologists call it the subconscious. It is the source of the primitive thought and is a very thin line between the Mental body and the Soul body, the Atma Sarup. It has the word *Baju* for chanting, and the sound is that of the buzzing of bees."[4]

Sing this word in contemplation, and see what happens—in daily life or in your dreams.

Part Three

―――――⌘―――――

The Supremacy of Love and Service

8
Love and Service

Sometimes I think back to some of the initiates who were in ECK years ago. I never quite figured out why they ever came to Eckankar. When I began mentioning Soul's goal of spiritual freedom and that the step beyond that was being a Co-worker with God, they said they were so tired of hearing the word service. They said they would have a fit if I said it one more time.

I said, "Boy, that's really tough because as long as I'm here, that's what I'm going to be talking about."

—Harold Klemp, *The Secret of Love*,
Mahanta Transcripts, Book 14[1]

---

*A*round June 1992, I had a Soul Travel experience in the dream state in which a priest of Eckankar visited me in the company of another ECKist.

You'll Be Helping Me!

As I escort them to the gate, the priest turns to me and says, "It looks like you'll be helping me from now on!" I think about it for a few seconds, then say, "Yeah!

179

It sure looks like that."

My sense of inadequacy for this assignment is reflected in the other ECKist. He looks at me and smirks, calling me an upstart.

A few months after this experience, my impromptu attendance at the ECK Worldwide Seminar would reveal the Master's way of training me for this mission I felt inadequate for!

Worldwide

A month or two after that dream, a High Initiate came to me—this time on the outer—and asked, "Have you considered going to the ECK Worldwide Seminar in Minneapolis this year?"

I hadn't. I had no money to travel, for one thing. The position of local-government chairman at that time was prestigious, yet the salary for the position barely met necessities. It certainly was not enough to travel to the United States. Considering how similar public officials treat public funds nowadays, some will wonder if I am referring to a chairmanship from another constellation in the universe. But this was true in my day.

Is it possible for me to attend this Worldwide? I asked the Mahanta.

The night I asked that question, I had a vivid dream of going to the seminar.

After that dream, people who owed me money from when I was a private architectural consultant came forward to settle debts I had all but written off. It was not long before I had enough money to attend the ECK Worldwide Seminar.

When I went to Kaduna for the visa interview, I had a powerful inner nudge: *Buy the flight ticket first, before you attend the visa interview.* So I did.

"Is the government sponsoring your trip?" asked the visa interviewer—a severe, no-nonsense lady—at the American consulate in Kaduna.

When I told her I was sponsoring myself, she warned me, "This is an expensive trip. How are you going to finance it?" Apparently, she didn't want to waste her time giving a visa to someone who couldn't afford the trip.

"Pull out the flight ticket and show her," the Inner Master said.

I pulled my KLM flight ticket from my bag and put it before her.

She took a long look at it and asked no more questions.

I got the visa.

This lady at the consulate apparently took the Law of Economy rather seriously. She gave me seven days' stay in the USA. At the US port of entry, they were more generous; I got three months. But six days later, I would be back in Nigeria, having beaten the visa officer's schedule by a day!

Training

In those days, I was yet to understand some of the secret ways the Mahanta uses in carrying out certain things. But years later, it occurred to me that at this Worldwide I had been trained for the position of local director even before I became a Second Initiate!

I met a very wonderful member of the Eckankar Spiritual Center staff, who gave me a ride to the Temple of ECK in Chanhassen. It was on condition that I agree to stay at the Temple of ECK for three hours—the time required to do his official duties there.

My stay for three hours at the Temple of ECK—a place of concentrated spirituality—was the first aspect of my training!

This fellow and his wife then took me to lunch. After lunch, this generous man organized a tour of the Eckankar Spiritual Center, the administrative hub of the ECK teachings in the world, just for me! It was the second phase of my training for the local leadership of Eckankar back home. But I did not realize this at the time.

On my way back to the venue of the seminar, I rode with Helen Baird—said to be one of the first chelas of Eckankar when Paul Twitchell brought out the modern teachings in 1965. She was also an Eighth Initiate. Apart from the driver, there were just the two of us in the car. It has been my regret ever since that I was too shy to exchange even a greeting with her!

I did not realize it yet, but this was the third aspect of my training.

The Dream Comes True

Three days after I got back to Nigeria, the ECK priest who had appeared in that Soul Travel experience and told me that I would be helping him from then on showed up at my house. Like in the dream experience, he was in the company of another ECKist.

As I escorted them to the gate, the High Initiate's approach differed a little from the dream state. Instead of speaking to me in the company of his companion, he called me aside.

"Plans are under way to split Benue State into three zones for the administration of Eckankar in Nigeria," he said. "If you are considered to lead this Gboko local area, would you accept?"

Out here in the physical, my feelings of inadequacy for the job loomed before me. I now saw why the Master had first made an inner approach from parallel worlds. There on the inner, I had accepted the assignment. Why should I refuse out here? So I accepted, and we shook hands on it.

Appointed

I was not yet a Second Initiate. So when I was appointed local director, I was called into a meeting I did not qualify to be in. Perhaps someone forgot or was unaware. However, my letter of appointment was delivered to me later outside the meeting room. I returned home with much hope of success in this endeavor. It looked easy.

I was mistaken.

The problems that awaited me in trying to establish Eckankar in my home area were perhaps harder than the proverbial "tough nut to crack." Would I be able to crack it at all?

Local Director

Prior to this time, ECKists in Gboko had rented a tiny room—just a little bigger than a cupboard—on one of the big roads in town, and there they would gather to sing HU. It was not adequate for an organization that was planning to grow. By the time I became local director, the landlord of this "cupboard" had given us quit notice anyway.

I had a dream about finding a new place, and we looked into another property this same landlord had just completed on the same road. But when we approached, the landlord had an opinion.

"No religious organizations, please!" was his curt answer.

We formed small, sometimes one-man, committees to look for a place where we could establish a base. There was always a vacancy till they learned who the would-be tenant was. Then, suddenly, the place would not be available.

For one full month, we combed the streets of Gboko, looking for appropriate places to create a home for the Mahanta's teachings about love. All we received were rejections and, sometimes, outright insults.

Good News

In January 1993, I got good news: a landlady was ready to rent to us.

"Did you explain to her who we are and exactly what we wanted the premises for?" I asked suspiciously. Even with so many rejections, I told members of the committee never to lie about who we were and what we were renting for.

"The lady said she would be most happy to rent her premises to Eckankar," our committee member said simply.

I went to meet her. She was all smiles, and I was surprised. *Could there be a story behind this?* I wondered.

There was. But until our rental contract expired two years later, I was none the wiser.

We paid our rent up front for two years and moved in after the decoration and furnishing were completed. Eckankar in Gboko finally had a home in Gboko North.

Quit Notice

Toward the end of our two years, we got three months' quit notice. The landlady would not renew.

Another exhausting house hunt filled those three months. All efforts turned out blank.

A week prior to our moving out, I had a dream about our next move. But the move suggested in the dream was so unusual that the meaning of the dream sailed over my head.

I go to visit the ECK center, which has been burgled and partly smashed up. Suspicious and hostile eyes from the neighborhood doors and windows follow me and my companions.

I find an eight-year-old girl on the site.

"You have an idea who ruined our ECK center?" I asked her. She has not responded yet, when a tall, rangy fellow appears on the site. He is one of those street marketers of audiocassettes; they walk along the streets carrying portable stereo cassette players and playing their music loudly to attract customers. The song this vendor was playing at top volume was a seventies hit by American pop star Al Green, "I Can't Get Next to You." After he had played this music for a while, people started to gather, and a market began to grow in the venue.

This dream had reflected both the present and the future.

The broken-up ECK center was evidence that the inner counterpart of our ECK center had already been removed. The young girl I met on site was our landlady. Her age in this dream reflected her true spiritual age (on the outer, she was approaching middle age). Al Green's song was Golden-tongued Wisdom about where the ECK center would set up home next. The market was the symbol for our next, more permanent, ECK center—nine years later!

Next to You

The Friday HU Chant was the last event of our two-year stay in this ECK center. After the event, I hopefully asked our house hunters whether anybody had been lucky. I had always thought somehow that the

Mahanta would come to our rescue at the very last moment. It was just a question of patience. It would end like all successful cliff-hangers: at the last moment, a new home would materialize.

But we had run out of luck.

I had thought about and dreaded this moment. But now here we were. And there were two alternatives open to me: either lay the idea of an ECK center in Gboko to rest or move it to the only place I could—my hired residence!

When I made the announcement of the temporary move of the ECK center into our family living room, even other ECKists were shocked. But no one had a better place to offer. There was simply no other choice.

The Move Was Right

On a Saturday, one night before the first ECK function would take place in our living room, I woke up there in a dream. Light was streaming through the windows, which seemed to have increased in number and size. A strong breeze wafted through the windows, making the curtains dance. It was the wind of ECK!

To me this was confirmation from the Mahanta that, in spite of the criticism of some people, the ECK said that the move was right.

The itinerant audiocassette seller in my dream had been the Mahanta. Through Al Green's song, the ECK had forewarned me that the ECK center was moving "next to you"—right into our family living room!

What of the future?

As the itinerant merchant played his cassettes, a market had begun to grow around the ECK center. This prediction was for the future.

When we finally found a place to rent for our ECK

center, the premises were opposite a market. It would have been useless trying to decipher this dream symbol at the time, since nine years separated the two ECK centers!

Former Landlady

Now, back to our former landlady. Why did she stop renting to us after two short years, when she had been so agreeable at first?

When the time came to vacate our former ECK center, our landlady started a very strange quarrel with us. According to her, there had been a security flood-light there when we moved in, but it was not there now that we were about to leave.

We called her several times to arrange meetings at the premises, but she would never turn up. Yet she would hang back in our absence and keep complaining about her missing floodlight, which none of us had seen. One day, she sent her agent to seize our billboard.

This action was most strange. Why our billboard?

A couple months after we had left—without our bill-board—someone who knew this woman very well came to me with the explanation of her strange behavior.

Our landlady and her husband had fallen out and were separated. This property had come into dispute between them. The man was about to go to court to press his claims. But the landlady was shrewd and knew her ex-husband's weakness.

She not only rented her property to Eckankar, seen by many in those days as a cult, but also dropped hints that she also was a member!

Relatives of the husband became alarmed and advised him to drop any claims on the property. Thus the ardor of the husband for the property cooled.

Our landlady had a respite for the two years that Eckankar stayed on her property. After these two years, the lady felt it was safe enough to reclaim her property from Eckankar. But just in case her husband began getting ideas, she had raised that false alarm about the missing floodlight and repeated her hints of being a member of Eckankar. To support those false claims, she retained our billboard to convince her husband that Eckankar had not moved out.

She kept the billboard displayed prominently at her window facing the main road for the whole length of time it took us to find a new ECK center. For nine years, while we searched, we got free advertisement! It was only after we found a new ECK center that the billboard disappeared from her picture window.

White Elephant?

A project doomed ab initio to failure, perhaps due to a poor feasibility study, is sometimes called a white elephant.

I had the following dream on Friday, March 22, 1998.

I am traveling through familiar terrain. I come upon a school established by a certain individual. The community had not approved the school, so it is considered a white elephant with little chance of succeeding. Even though a well-beaten path leads to the school, none leads away from the school grounds. It's like the compound of a miser who refuses to have a road running through his property lest a stranger happen by during mealtime.

This dream haunted me for a while. It seemed to reflect the grudging toleration or outright nonacceptance of the teachings of Eckankar in Gboko since we had started, six years earlier.

Community Approval

I have just told about the problems we had renting a place for an ECK center. At the time I had this dream, the ECK center was still in our family living room—not out of choice, but out of necessity.

Was the introduction of Eckankar in Gboko—something I had assumed as a personal responsibility given to me by the Mahanta—doomed to become a white elephant?

One comfort I had was that this dream had a second, hopeful part to it.

I get to a river crossing that is actually some kind of rapids with powerful currents. I am in the company of two others, one a family member.

After deciding where we will land on the other side, we jump in. The current is much stronger than I had expected. My family member gives me concern—will she make it? She does, after what proves to be a hair-raising swim across. We land farther downstream than we had expected.

We Need to Work at This

I decided that the crossing of the river in this part of the dream meant the establishment of the ECK center. It would take a hard swim—a lot of work. And we would not end up where we had expected, but we would succeed all the same.

Someone on transfer from Lagos arrived on the scene when it became imperative for me to move back to the state capital. He agreed that the ECK center could move into his residence while we continued to search for a suitable place. But I had no intention of leaving the fledgling community of ECKists with the onerous task of seeing that the ECK teachings succeeded in Gboko.

At the time I returned to the state capital, however,

my car became too expensive for me to maintain and I had to sell it. Without a car, my travel plans had to become more creative in order to keep going to ECK events in Gboko.

Buses and taxis in Nigeria do not operate according to rigid schedules as they do in some other parts of the world. The time for the bus to move is when the vehicle has filled up—sometimes beyond its capacity! Because of this, I had to get up around four or four-thirty in the morning on Sundays to get to the motor park early enough to board the first taxi going to Gboko. Otherwise I might be late for the ECK Worship Service or discussion class.

Encouraged

In April 2003, I attended the first ECK Spiritual Skills Seminar, in Washington, DC. One of my three goals for this seminar was to find a way to get a proper place for an ECK center in Gboko. A workshop titled "Doing Big Things in a Small Area" attracted me, and I attended.

As I had expected, the workshop was conceived to address the problems of ECKists who lived in a small community but who nonetheless wanted to serve the Mahanta in that tight corner of the world. This suited me fine.

I sat next to an American lady.

"How many ECKists do you have in your area?" she asked me when I told her the reason for my attending this workshop.

"It fluctuates," I said. "Sometimes it's five, other times eight."

"You *are* lucky!" she said, surprising me. In the state where she came from, she and her husband formed the entire ECK community! The ECK had placed me next to a person whose situation was worse than mine. It might sound unkind, but I felt encouraged.

Not About to Hide

When I returned from that seminar, I had a dream in which I had returned with a blue tool kit for the administration of Eckankar. This, I knew, was renewed love of the Mahanta.

Soon after, someone approached me. A certain political party that had lost an election was moving out of a prominent place on a busy road—one of our firm specifications for an ECK-center location. We were not about to hide in some secret corner of town. This place, when I saw it, suited us fine. It was public and prominent.

Even Eckankar Is in Town!

We approached the landlord and were explicit on the reason why we wanted to hire.

"My place is your place!" he said, singling me out. We agreed on the rent and settled it for one year up front. The renovations and furnishing came next. I also got one of the top sign makers in town to create the exacting and imposing signboard for the ECK center, and we hung it outside.

Some time later, I learned that the pastor of a large Protestant church had unwittingly confirmed the establishment of our new ECK center. Disappointed with the lukewarm responses to his church's fund-raisers, he said to his congregation, "If you are unhappy where you are, go to where you will be happy. There is freedom now. Even Eckankar is in town!"

Whatever his intent, his comment confirmed the good news to me:

Eckankar is not a white elephant in Gboko after all!

Salary Arrears

I cannot recall where the Master wrote that service is its own reward, but I once reaped a humorous reward from serving others unselfishly. I became famous through happenstance!

Financial Quagmire

When I started off as chairman, our local government had inherited a huge bill of salary arrears from my predecessor. Most of these salary arrears were owed to primary-school teachers, and our local government had the largest number in the state.

The affairs of primary schools had once been in the care of the federal government in Nigeria. Somewhere around the late eighties, the military president unloaded the affairs of primary schools on the local governments. He made marginal increases in allocations of funds from oil revenues to the local governments to take care of their increased responsibility for the primary-school teachers' salaries. These changes produced no serious problems for rural-based local governments that did not have many primary schools. However, our local government had a large urban population, and the cost of primary schools, even with the marginal increase in financing, had resulted in a net loss of close to one quarter of our revenue!

How did my immediate predecessor tackle this shortfall?

Liabilities

For the three months in which he served, he simply ignored paying teachers' salaries. He treated the teachers as if they didn't exist. One month prior to his departure, he also ignored the leave bonuses of the rest of the local-government staff. Then he dramatically increased the staff by employing people, mainly from his area, and off-loading them on the new administration!

I have no idea how he tackled the leadership of the labor unions, but they never called for a strike even once. By the time I came in, the treasury was empty and there were millions of naira worth of liabilities. These included the three months' salary arrears for the teaching staff, the month's worth of leave bonuses for all the staff, and another huge bill to contractors. On top of it all, there were the wages for our bloated staff.

The place was a keg of gunpowder waiting to explode!

Ways Out

With much support from the politicians, some of whom already suspected the sad state of affairs that had been bequeathed to us, we of the local-government council huddled together and began to map ways out of the financial quagmire.

Within eight months, to even my personal surprise, we wiped out the arrears bequeathed from our predecessor!

As these salary arrears began to pour out to the teaching staff, the Central Bank of Nigeria released, for the first time, the fifty-naira note—the highest denomination of Nigerian currency at the time. The national heroes pictured on the banknote were nameless ordinary Nigerians. This was in contrast to other banknotes in Nigeria, each of which bore the name and picture of a famous national hero.

Street Name of Fifty-Naira Note

One day, a political colleague from an adjoining local government visited. As he left, I helped with his transport fare. The money I gave him was in the form of the new fifty-naira notes. He took a look at the notes and chuckled.

"Do you know the street name for this banknote?" he asked. I told him I didn't.

"Jon Uan—that's the name of this banknote on the streets!"

Though we both laughed, I took this with a grain of salt till I left public office and began to move more freely on the streets. Wherever I went in the Benue community from the Tiv-speaking area in Nigeria, the fifty-naira banknote was indeed called the Jon Uan! Many market women called out the name freely, without the slightest idea that the man whose name they were using was there among them. It was very amusing.

Many friends called to ask me how this had come about. At fund-raisers, they had heard people saying that so-and-so has donated so many Jon Uans.

Mystified

I was mystified myself, so I decided to research the story.

Some people were of the opinion that during my chairmanship, I used to scoop these notes from my pocket and, without counting them, give them out as gifts to visitors. This, I knew, was not true. We operated under such a stringent budget to meet our basic needs that there was no room for such profligacy. As a matter of fact, by the time I left the chairmanship, I was worse off financially than when I had gone in.

One day, I got a far more plausible explanation from the wife of an associate who ran a local open-air restaurant.

During the three months when the teachers had not been paid their salaries, many had bought their meals on credit from her. She knew that many other food sellers, including those who sold raw food items and groceries, had been selling on credit to a lot of teachers. At the end of three months, the teachers were getting close to the limit of their credit when the arrears payments began to arrive.

Coincidentally, it was during the payment of these salary arrears that the Central Bank of Nigeria released the fifty-naira banknote.

Many of these teachers did not have bank accounts; they took their salaries in cash—with the new notes, of course! The good-hearted ones rushed over to the market women to settle their grocery bills with the freshly minted—and strange—banknotes.

"Mama-Put (as these food sellers are called in Nigeria) take. This is from the Jon Uan arrears!"

The name stuck.

There were thousands of these teachers in every nook and corner of the local-government jurisdiction, including the rural areas, rushing over to pay their food bills with the new banknote. Since there was no specific national hero pictured on it, the teachers and market women made an impromptu decision to create one. I became the "victim."

Famous through a Coincidence

Overnight, I had become famous through a silly coincidence!

One of the greatest rewards a politician craves is fame and recognition. It eases the process of standing for elective office, as one doesn't have to spend time explaining who he or she is.

Even though my road to fame was silly, it was real and politically useful.

When the movement to ease the military out of power

started, we hit the road to sell our political party to the people. A huge round of applause always greeted me when I was introduced by the MC in any part of the state, particularly in the large Tiv-speaking area. Some never believed Jon Uan was a real human being, much less a living one. After all, no famous national hero pictured on Nigerian currency is alive!

When I sweated through those eight months to bring about financial order in the affairs of the local government, I was just doing a difficult job the best way I could. I had no idea this would bring fame of this nature to me. *Service is its own reward*, I thought. But later this fame would also help put a local face—for those who needed it—on the teachings of Eckankar in our area.

Dream Journals

My dream journals grew richer and more complex every day, and I began to get this nudge that one day I might publish something from them as service to the Mahanta. But I had a worry.

What to Share?

"How does the Law of Silence apply to stories like this?" I asked the Mahanta.

The response to my question took me by surprise, and it came almost immediately in a Soul Travel experience.

It started as a dream, and I knew just where I was in this dream. No one told me in so many words, but as so often happens in these experiences, nobody has to hold up a sign and say this is where you are. You just know!

And I just knew that I was in the Katsupari Monastery in the Buika Magna mountain range of northern Tibet.

Katsupari Monastery

People I assume to be ECK Masters are seated inside a large room. In their midst stands the white-bearded abbott of the monastery, Fubbi Quantz, an ECK Master. In his hand he holds a book. It has a mostly sky-blue cover. The title of the book is The Living ECK Master at My Side. *In his distinctive voice, he tells the gathered assembly that the ECK Masters mandated him to write the book he now holds in his hand.*

"The Mahanta's mission in this spiritual era," he says, "is to carry the teachings of Eckankar to all nooks and corners of creation. All these writings are to help with that mission.

What Are You Waiting For?

"What are you waiting for?" Fubbi Quantz's eyes blaze in my direction like twin torches.

Startled, I look on stupidly, then realize that he is now addressing me!

I have been standing on the fringes of this assembly, thinking that I was here strictly as an observer and not an active participant.

"What are you waiting for?" he asks once again. "Begin writing!" he commands, addressing me directly.

I knew immediately, when I woke up, that I had to dig for stories inside my dream journals—stories that demonstrated how the relationship of the student with the Living ECK Master could help the former to keep stepping along spiritually.

The stories are very personal, yet with some effort on the reader's part, they go to show that divine love can be easily accessed through God's principal channel in heaven and on earth—the Mahanta!

Try this spiritual exercise today!

More Than Just Getting By

Pick one day a week where you will do more than just get by. On that day put your whole heart into taking care of your family, your work, and yourself.

So many people spend their lives just trying to get by. That's all they really want to do. A person like that isn't material for God Consciousness; his cloth is different from one who is striving for the highest spiritual states.

People of the golden heart care about things. They are filled with love, they finish what they start, and they like to see it done well.

—Sri Harold Klemp
The Spiritual Exercises of ECK[2]

9

Wisdom

"The ECKist knows nothing and does nothing of himself; he is quiet and lets the ECK act through him in Its power. He takes no pay in any form—neither fame, nor service, nor property, nor personal power—and since he does not, they all come to him. This is the way that It works in man, which is the natural vehicle for Its power."

—*The Shariyat-Ki-Sugmad*, Books One & Two[1]

Some might ask, why should one ask God for advice in a common situation such as whom to marry? But I had cause to. My own personal decisions had failed me once too often. Before the age of forty years, I had suffered three failed marriages.

That kind of scorecard should make one humble. You can't just keep blaming the other partner for all that failure. At least part of the blame was mine. Where did it come from?

Who Should I Marry?

None of my earlier marriages had lasted beyond three years. Now, at the age of forty-two, I was once again between marriages. Although I was with some-

one I planned to marry, the relationship was not perfect. But what relationship is?

Then I met my present wife.

She was twenty-two years my junior—not my type
at all. But soon enough, I began to see qualities in her
that were lacking in the woman I had a long-term relationship with. Something told me I should explore
this new relationship. But old habits die hard.

Fortunately at this time, I was also looking into the
teachings of Eckankar, which encourage trust in God
rather than our emotions and mind.

I had been wrong three times. What did I have to
lose by letting a superior, spiritual intelligence decide
for me?

God Did Not Speak from the Clouds

One evening, I sat down and said, "God, I am confused. Of these two women, who should I marry?"

God did not speak from the clouds. But the lady I
had been planning to marry spoke. And she spoke clearly
and plenty!

In the ensuing two weeks, she began to exhibit,
with the most incredible clarity, the differences that
would come between us after we married. These differences had been there all along, but they had never been
displayed so clearly. It was now much easier deciding
whom to marry.

One Size Does Not Fit All

My former marriages failed, and I hadn't been able
to marry my first fiancée. I now realized that the reason was not that they were bad people.

Marriage partners are like shoes—one size does not
fit all. Just because the shoe does not fit one person, it
does not mean that it will not fit another.

I had been blinded by habit and age difference. So the Master showed me in practical ways how the "older shoe" would pinch me if "purchased."

I discovered that with the younger woman the Mahanta had brought me a "shoe" that fitted me better. Fifteen years of a successful marriage still going strong have proved this.

I am glad I listened.

Resort-Hotel Project

A lesson I needed to learn was:

If you want their cooperation, put yourself in the shoes of the people you deal with.

In other words, forget the ego if you want to succeed.

I was appointed as consultant on a project for a wildlife resort hotel. The client was one of the state governments in Nigeria. The commissioner for Wildlife and Forest Resources stood like an angry rhino between me and the progress of the project. He was wearing me thin, and he knew it.

At My Tether's End

Every time I completed and presented the preliminary designs for his approval, he would find some "major fault" which would necessitate a complete overhaul of the design. Sometimes the changes he made were the very things he had introduced himself previously!

This was before the days of computer-aided design (CAD). All these alterations had to be done by hand. The cost, in both materials and man-hours, was wearing me thin.

After the fifth presentation and rejection, I was at my tether's end.

I Put Myself in His Place

Before the next presentation attempt, I had a nudge to put myself in the place of the honorable commissioner. What was his interest here? What was his mindset, and how could I satisfy it and still do my job? Then I asked God for help.

Just that quickly, the answer stood clearly before me. I wondered why I had not seen it before. Perhaps I had spent too much time being angry to notice.

The honorable commissioner had once been a dashing young man. However, age and illness, perhaps due to hard living, had caught up with him. Consciously or not, he knew that he was gradually losing command of both his body and life around him. Perhaps for reassurance, he displayed several photographs of himself that had been taken when he was looking much better. He also had a retinue of political sycophants whom he allowed to hang around in his office and at home. Their job was to assure the aging and sick man that he was OK; he was still a great man.

The photographs and sycophants never failed in this. Both were always there when I made my presentations. They applauded the clever commissioner as he made this "architectural snob" jump through the hoops.

When it came to architecture, the man couldn't tell the difference between an arch and starch. Yet he enjoyed twisting me around to entertain his sycophants. The honorable commissioner had little interest in the project or its designer's abilities. He therefore used my presentations to preen himself before his favorite audience.

You can let his own ego win him over! the Inner Master hinted.

Surrender of My Anger

After a little thought, I knew just how to do that. I would do my job very well, but after that, I would forget about it. From there on, I would assist with the commissioner's preening exercise.

On the sixth presentation I found the usual audience—mobile and immobile—waiting in the commissioner's office. This time, I brought two stacks of drawings. One stack was big and unruly, while the other was orderly and small.

"Chief," I started with enthusiasm, "you should have studied architecture. I have learned so much from you."

With that kind of opening, the place went silent. A side glance confirmed that the sycophants sat in the lounging chairs and were listening in. But the commissioner looked over to them and cleared his throat to make sure he had their attention.

It's Your Design, Chief!

"I have two stacks of drawings on this table," I said, pointing. "This large stack here is the rubbish I included in the earlier designs, which you rightly rejected." With that, I swept the untidy stack of drawings off the desk and let them rustle to the floor.

"And this heap here," I continued, caressing the drawings that remained on the table, "are the golden lines that you had distilled from all that garbage I had produced. Everything here is exactly as you have wanted. It's your design, Chief!"

Throughout this presentation, the man was nodding at every word.

The presentation I gave that day was not about how well I had designed the project, but what the commissioner had done to make it a masterpiece. He was unlikely to destroy his own masterpiece! But I was still somehow apprehensive as I awaited his response.

Approved!

The commissioner pushed his glasses down his nose and scanned the drawings. He kept nodding as he did. I knew these nods had nothing to do with his comprehension of the intricate design. It was more of a show put on for the benefit of the silent listeners. *The chief has finally educated an architect to the latter's duties!* they were probably thinking.

"Approved!" he ejaculated like a king giving assent to a decree he had ordered drafted.

The audience duly clapped. I did too—more out of relief than admiration.

I walked home singing a little tune.

Wisdom, as I observed earlier, is for the humble. When we forget that and carry around a big ego ourselves, the ECK, or Holy Spirit, often sends someone who is even more desperate in this shortcoming than we are to teach us a lesson—the way the commissioner taught me mine.

Mother of All Contracts

Of all the decisions I made as local-government chairman, perhaps the one I savor most concerns what I call the Mother of All Contracts. Basically, someone tried to get me to misuse the power of my office to benefit him, just so he could score a point. But once I asked for help from the Mahanta, the ensuing solution surprised us both!

People He Could Use

For the protection of his identity, let me call him Andy.

Andy not only loved trouble, he thrived on it. He always had in his company a lot of street urchins called *area boys* in Nigeria. He often sent these boys to settle his scores when he had a tiff with anybody. For this reason, he was a feared man.

When it became clear that I would likely be elected at the local-government polls, Andy joined my campaign team. His reasons for joining were twofold.

For one thing, he knew I was likely to win. Andy didn't care much for losers. He only associated with people he could use.

There are very few politicians who don't have ears and eyes at their back. Because of this, I discovered the second reason why Andy hitched his wagon to my star.

Andy equated my quiet, considerate ways to weak leadership. He figured I could be pressured into serving *his* interests once I was in office.

Miscalculated

However, once I got into office, Andy discovered, to his chagrin, that he had miscalculated. He wasn't getting the patronage he had hoped for. His first attack was to publicly call me names, hoping that I would respond.

I didn't.

Not getting a reaction from me made Andy furious.

Next, the rumor bearers began to bring snippets of insults from Andy against my person. Andy was sending these emissaries to me, hoping for a reaction.

"If Andy wakes up one day and stops doing what he is doing," I told his emissaries, "I will become worried, thinking that something untoward has befallen him!"

It was a reaction from me, but not the one Andy had hoped for. He had wanted me to start a battle. But I knew that Andy, like all professional troublemakers, felt like a fish out of water when there was no trouble or controversy to thrive on.

Soon enough, Andy got his theater to press for his dream.

Not Just Any Contract

I discovered that the local-government's secretary of education, without consulting me, gave a contract to Andy. And it was not just any contract.

The local government's main sports stadium sat next to a primary school which was also an institution of the local government. During a football match, youth who could not afford the gate fee climbed onto the roof of the classroom block nearest the sports facility to watch. Their combined weight was too much, and the roof collapsed.

Now, this was not an ordinary primary school. It was the alma mater of the paramount chief of the area, many high-ranking military officers (retired and active), and a retinue of other VIPs. And they still took an active interest in the affairs of the school.

The school block, moreover, was next to a very popular road named after the first paramount ruler of the locale. The high and mighty had expressed concerns, and they desired that the repairs be effected forthwith. And now the secretary of education, without referring the matter to me, had awarded the contract to Andy. The latter now had the connection he needed to rile me.

I learned through the political grapevine that Andy planned to collect the mobilization fees, then take a walk—a popular action at one point in the life of Nigerians. A person of influence gets a contract, collects the mobilization fees, and walks away.

"I'd like to see the dog that would try to come after me," Andy was said to have threatened.

I knew I was the dog Andy was referring to.

Political Solution

People who live in politically stable cultures, where the rule of law works even with the high and mighty, might find it hard to comprehend a situation such as this. How could a man commit a crime and just thumb his nose at the law simply because he had certain political weight behind him? But this sort of thing is not strange to Nigeria.

In fact, a civilian political godfather once used the police to take a state governor hostage, trying to force him to resign! It was tantamount to a coup and kidnapping. Yet, the civilian was never arrested. Instead, the high and mighty in the ruling party asked for a "political solution." The case never made it to the court of law but was settled by a committee within the ruling party!

If Andy collected mobilization fees for a contract from the local government and took a walk—and particularly if he shared such loot with the right people—handing him over to the police would have led nowhere. There would have been an outcry for a "political solution"—in other words, a decision to let him go. If I had insisted that the right thing be done, the ensuing controversy would have given Andy the public theater he so craved. He would use it to strike out at the current government and show how heartless it was.

The only thing I could do was try to ensure that no pay went out until the work was done.

No Pay Up Front

I called a meeting of the Education Department and the cash office.

"Anybody who pays Andy one kobo up front will find himself out of this local government!" I said. "Do I make myself clear?"

When Andy heard about this decision, he said he

would never start the job without mobilization fees. And if we dared revoke the contract and award it to another, he would mobilize his area boys to beat and harass the new contractor on site and ensure that the job was never completed.

He did not say it, but he must certainly have thought, *If you take me to the police, so much the better.* That would give him the public theater he craved.

Graceful Way

For three months, this collapsed roof sat like a gaping wound, weighing on the conscience of the local government. When some of the high-classed alumni, who had no knowledge of the imbroglio dogging the project, began asking why this school block remained that way, Andy was pleased. The waiting game favored him.

Or did it?

One day, I turned to the Inner Master.

"What is the most graceful way out of this situation?" I asked at bedtime.

I got no dream that night to show me the way out. But the next day, instead of a dream, the Mahanta sent a real solution!

Thunderclap!

An elderly woman I knew barged into my office. This abrasive woman's presence always brought apprehension. She was a tough character with a loud voice to match. We nicknamed her Thunderclap—secretly, of course!

As usual, Thunderclap was full of fire.

"When I die," she spat, "those who are not providing succor while I am alive should never come to shed crocodile tears at my funeral with false donations!"

In the past, such tirades were irritants. But today, I smiled, and the smile was authentic.

"Come back tomorrow, madam, and I will offer you a contract that gives you that succor you speak about so often."

She stopped short and eyed me suspiciously, to see if I was putting her on. But I believe she saw no guile in my face, for the simple reason that there was none. Today, Thunderclap was welcome to my office—for a good reason.

When she left, I picked up the phone and dialed the secretary of education.

"Revoke Andy's contract," I said, "and give it to Thunderclap."

There was silence at the other end for a few seconds, and then the silence gave way to a roar of laughter.

"It'll be done right away, boss," said the relieved secretary.

He had given Andy that contract in good faith. It was a shock and embarrassment to him that Andy was using it to hold the local government to ransom.

Sound of Hammering

Next morning, when I drove past the school, I heard the sound of hammering. Carpenters were working on that building's roof.

That was quick! I thought. *Has Thunderclap started already?*

When I had settled down in the office, I dialed the secretary of education. He answered right away.

"Has Thunderclap started already?" I asked.

The secretary convulsed into laughter. "It's not her; it's Andy's team."

"How come? He said he wouldn't start without mobilization fees."

"He discovered he had run out of alternatives," the secretary said, laughing.

Andy discovered he had two choices open to him—fulfill the contract or send his area boys to beat up Thunderclap.

The second option was no alternative at all.

He would have become the most famous man in town for the wrong reason—beating up his own mother-in-law. Because that was who Thunderclap was!

As soon as I had asked for divine help, a string of funny "coincidences" came my way.

It was perfect timing, and even Andy must have got the picture.

Promises Kept

On the day the inspection team approved the completion of the job, I ordered that Andy be paid in full immediately.

He should have been pleased, but Andy was enraged. He didn't cherish someone getting the better of him in this manner. His insults against me increased, but they had no power, particularly when people began to make fun of him. "Why are you bothering the chairman when you were floored by your own mother-in-law?" they would ask.

What of my promise to Thunderclap?

She made an appearance the next day, as scheduled.

We somehow sourced a contract for her. It was not as juicy as the other one, but I had never been explicit as to the type of contract I was going to give her. Once she got the contract, Thunderclap uncharacteristically smiled and thanked me.

You have no idea of the thanks I owe you, I thought, *for letting me hide behind your skirts—or wrapper, as the case may be—from Andy.*

I think this was the most pleasing and aesthetic solution of my tenure as chairman. And, except to Andy, the solution also had humor—certainly a nice addendum to the path of wisdom and humility.

Try this spiritual exercise today!
— ❦ —

Viewing Difficulties

In contemplation, look at your problem and ask yourself which of these viewpoints you hold about it.

1. You view the problem as a battering ram. When it approaches, you fall over backward, flattened to the ground.

2. You view the problem as a vital, valuable lesson which will teach you something. You believe it will become a spiritual springboard to give you the necessary incentive and energy to climb up and out of your present situation.

Your attitude about your problem holds the key to whether your experience with it will be easy or difficult, long or short.

Those people who have spiritual success don't say, "Oh no!" and fall down when a problem comes up. They look to see the reason or the lesson behind it. They ask the Mahanta, "What can I learn from it? How has it made me stronger?"

—Sri Harold Klemp
The Spiritual Exercises of ECK[2]

10

The Gift of HU

The word HU *is the Spirit of all sounds and of
all words, and is hidden under them all as the
Spirit of Soul. It does not belong to any language;
no language can help belonging to it. This alone
is the true name of God, a name that no people
and no religion can claim as their own. This
word is not only uttered by human beings but it
is repeated by animals and birds.*

—Paul Twitchell, *The Flute of God*[1]

---

*H*e was powerfully built. He had migrated
from Benue State to Taraba to work a
farm. But no matter how hard he worked,
he seemed not to make progress in his life. He was
always running into freak accidents and bad luck. He
said someone, somewhere, had told him that Eckankar
could help him.

Snake Charmer

At the time we met, a room in my residence was still
doubling as the ECK center.

While he spoke, I sang HU silently, asking the

213

Inner Master to let me be a clear instrument of Divine Spirit. A question came to mind, and I asked it.

"Do you recall any dreams when you sleep?" I asked him.

"Yes, I do. But in these dreams I encounter snakes wherever I turn. I can't move around in my dreams because I fear snakebite."

"I don't have an antidote to your problem," I told him. "But would you want me to give you a special prayer to try in the privacy of your room?"

Sing HU

He said he would like that very much. So I taught him how to sing HU, and we sang it together. I encouraged him to continue singing HU back at home.

He returned in about three months' time.

"How has it been?" I asked him.

"The snakes are still there in my dreams," he said. "But ever since I began singing HU, I find myself floating above these snakes. They cannot harm me!"

No Book? No Problem!

When I returned from the ECK African Seminar held in Lagos in July 1991, I was carrying higher spiritual energy than usual because of the meeting with the Master at the seminar. But I was unaware of this.

My sister must have picked up on it, though.

Our powerful matriarch of a grandmother had prevented our parents from sending my sister to school; she never got to go. But when I returned from the seminar in Lagos, she began to hound me.

"What's this thing called Eckankar?" she kept asking.

Why I Kept Mum

I kept mum for two reasons.

As I explained in chapter 2, when I had the experience with the Master as "Mr. Fireflies" in Lagos and could not find an appropriate religious organization in which to express what I felt inside, I left the Protestant faith of my youth and pitched camp with the Catholics. My sister was still with the Protestants. Any mention of my new religion had always brought a conflict between us, even though we loved each other so much. Now I thought that if Catholicism, another face of Christianity, brought such a storm of conflict between us, wouldn't Eckankar raise a hurricane?

The second reason was that I was new to the teachings of ECK. I had not made them such a part of my experience that I would be able to explain them to her in our native language. All I could do in those days was rehash what I had read—in English, of course—in the ECK books. My sister had no command of English and would not understand.

But for three days running, she wouldn't quit. One evening, close to six o'clock, she called at the house once more.

"Why won't you tell me something about this Eckankar?"

"We're about to do a family HU song," I told her. "You can join us if you wish."

I never bothered to explain what she should expect during this HU song.

We sang HU for about twenty minutes. After that, she turned rather quiet and never asked me a single question. Instead, she said good-bye and left.

Incredible Story

Next day, she returned with an incredible story.

During the HU song, she said a ball of blue light,

like a balloon, appeared before her forehead. With every outgoing breath, the blue balloon expanded, and then it contracted every time she took another deep breath. When the outer singing of the HU song ended, the sound of the HU song inside her did not stop! It almost drowned out the outer sounds. By the time she walked out onto the road to go back to her house, the HU sound reverberating within was so loud that she had to be careful not to be run over, since she could barely hear the motor vehicles coming!

Out of the Body

That night, she went to bed early. As she lay in bed with her face toward the wall, trying to sleep, it appeared as if the wall had opened. Then she saw a man with a thick, short-cropped beard spring out of the wall. His body seemed to be created out of a million tiny stars. And he was smiling.

Welcome! He had sent a mute but clearly understood impression to her. Then he shook her hand, held it, and drew her out of her body!

Where they stood, many moons and other planets hung low in the sky. Then it appeared as if a red liquid had come out of a lightbulb in her room and fallen on the floor. She looked at the floor for the stain it must have made. There was none.

This man held her hand, and they began to ascend. Very soon, she began to hear a church bell.

Has someone passed away? she wondered.

In the culture of her church, they always rang the church bell when a member had died. Could *she* have died? She wondered about that, and panic started setting in.

That quickly, she was reunited with her body!

Pictures

After the Lagos seminar, I had brought back a number of pictures of the ECK Masters. "If you saw a picture of the man you met," I asked her, "could you identify him?"

She said she could.

My wife went and brought the six pictures of ECK Masters I had brought back from Lagos. She placed them in front of my sister.

Without the slightest hesitation, she picked Rebazar Tarzs's picture. "It's him," she said. "That's the man who came and took me out of the body. The only difference is that, in the dream, his body seemed to be made of millions of stars!"

More Open Than Us

My sister proved to be more open to meeting these ECK Masters than we were. We had been mainly just reading about them in books. When I saw that she was so open to these inner worlds, I recalled having read that even in the inner worlds, there were crooks. So I advised her, "If you meet anyone on the inner, and you feel uneasy, challenge them. Ask them, 'In the name of Sugmad, who are you?'"

Challenge

My sister had said before that whenever she encountered these ECK Masters in her dreams, they brought with them a good feeling. But one day, when she sat singing HU, two people appeared, and she did not feel the usual buoyant feeling she felt in the presence of the ECK Masters.

"In the name of Sugmad, who are you?" she had challenged.

Immediately the two figures dissolved like mist. In their place, a stout, completely bald-headed man swam into view. His large eyes were reflecting all the colors of a rainbow, and she felt at peace in his presence. When we again showed her pictures of the ECK Masters, she identified the man as Yaubl Sacabi.

Without Book Knowledge

My sister, without book knowledge, had better access to the ECK Masters than I who had been reading about them.

Seeing the ECK Masters on the inner planes is assurance that one has encountered the Light and Sound of God—Divine Spirit—which is the supreme teacher of Soul. And that's all one needs to make spiritual progress.

My unschooled sister was at peace with these encounters. This was in complete contrast to a university professor I knew. He had quite a different experience because he let his intellectual pride stand between him and the help of the ECK Masters.

Plenty Book? Plenty Problem!

The professor was a former school colleague. I went into architectural practice, but he pursued a career that eventually led to the academic pinnacle—a university professor's chair.

The professor paid me a visit at my official residence and asked me what Eckankar was all about. After hearing my explanation he wanted to borrow an ECK book.

Hardest Book

"Bring the hardest book—absolutely the hardest—that Eckankar has to offer."

His attitude was understandable.

In all of his professional life, the professor had been fed on a diet of mental gymnastics—the stock-in-trade of academia. He thought the strange teachings he imagined Eckankar to be were no different—some mystic puzzle from the East to be demolished by that superior mind of his.

I lent him *The Golden Heart*, Mahanta Transcripts, Book 4. This book is a compilation of seminar talks by the spiritual leader of Eckankar. In these talks, Sri Harold Klemp often uses stories from life to illustrate how we can open our hearts more to the love of God—the only way to make true spiritual progress.

Reading about how to develop a more loving heart was not hard for me. *Becoming* a loving heart was absolutely the hardest thing I knew of—and a lot of ECKists would agree. As far as I was concerned, I had given the hardest ECK book to the professor.

Events of the next day, however, proved that he was not impressed.

This Is Water

"This is water," he complained as he returned the book.

True to his calling, the professor had read the entire book overnight and declared it to be nothing but diluted water—if such a thing were possible.

"Perhaps you didn't get me," he said. "I wanted the hardest, most difficult book Eckankar has to offer."

How could I get it through to the professor that the hard part was not inside any book but inside his heart?

Thinking that size might impress and slow the professor down so he would contemplate a little on what he read, I gave him the nearly four-hundred-page *How to*

Find God, Mahanta Transcripts, Book 2.

"This is a large book, Professor," I told him. "It might help a lot if you ask the Master who wrote it to help you comprehend it."

Attitude

"Bah!" the professor spat. "I don't need a master. Just hand over the book."

"If you have no need for a master, that's fine," I said. "But when you want to see the other side of this book, which is there but is invisible to your human eyes, sing this song, and you might just see it." Then I introduced the professor to the HU song.

The professor took at least two days this time to return. When he did, it was without the familiar swagger he was known for. He was like the fellow who had come looking for a secret-society encounter out of curiosity and got more than he had bargained for.

Strange Question

In almost a whisper, he asked, "Do you think I am going to die?"

It was such a strange question that I looked into his face to be sure he was not putting me on. Theatrics was part of his professional calling. But the professor was not into theatrics just now. He definitely had a problem.

"What happened?" I asked.

"The book is still watery," he said, "but the experience is not!"

"What experience?" I was now quite curious.

Out-of-Body Experience

As usual, the professor had whipped through the four hundred pages in one evening. Perhaps his reading of this book so soon after the other had a spiritually cumulative effect.

Once he finished this second book, he sat down to sing HU and try to discover the invisible side of the book I had spoken about. Suddenly he was out of the body in full consciousness "with a pull at the Spiritual Eye that felt like when a fish takes the hook of a fishing line," to use his own words.

One moment, he was singing HU on the comfortable settee in his bedroom; in the next moment, there was a pull at his Spiritual Eye, and he found himself in a dense jungle!

A Hostile Place

This jungle was absolutely the most hostile place he had ever been in or ever read about.

Wild tribesmen with poisoned arrows were behind every tree. A helicopter gunship hovered above, firing missiles through any opening in the thick canopy of foliage. Wild animals, including poisonous snakes and boa constrictors, lay in wait at every turn.

A part of him knew that his body was safe inside his bedroom, singing what he had assumed to be a nonsensical word. But here he was in this jungle with no idea how to get out alive.

When he at last returned to his physical body, the professor discovered he had been out for seven hours! It had felt like seven years. After this experience, he was not sure if his physical body would survive.

"You think I am going to die?" he repeated, looking at me with a plea in his eyes.

Help Available

"No, you're not going to die, Professor."

There was immediate relief in his face.

I explained to him that the jungle he went into was the invisible inner counterpart of his own world—the world he has created with his emotions, actions, and thoughts as an individual.

His eyebrows shot up, but he was speechless.

I also assured him that the ECK Masters were available to help him safely through the jungle of his state of consciousness.

"Remember, you said you did not need a master," I reminded him. "The ECK Masters never intervene if not invited. To use a Nigerian expression, ECK Masters never 'put hand or mouth' when not invited."

It was, therefore, entirely the prerogative of the professor to remain in the jungle of his own creation for seven hours—or seven days, weeks, years, or even seven more lifetimes—if he so chose.

Not Ready

Apparently, "You're not going to die" was the only gospel the professor was ready for at that moment. He quietly handed the book back to me and never asked for another ECK book—hard or watery, then or later.

In fact, in our subsequent meetings, he never broached the topic about that experience. He behaved almost as if it never happened. Perhaps he was afraid even a brief discussion of it might take him back to that jungle of his inner life.

No Book, No Problem

I recalled the inner experiences my sister had shared. She had never had any formal education but fared very well with her inner experiences.

In comparison, the professor seemed not to fare as well, though he had a great academic background. The so-called illiterate seemed more at home in her inner worlds or heavens than a man of great learning did in his. I am not suggesting that this is always the case, though.

Book knowledge alone does not open the door to heaven. Singing the HU does.

One does not have to go to school to learn to sing HU. If you or someone you know is thinking of coming into Eckankar, and there are worries about lack of literacy or education, stop worrying.

Remember, No book, no problem!

Try this spiritual exercise today!

⟡

What Is HU?

Singing HU or chanting your secret word enhances your life and gives you strength. HU is a holy name for God which will lift you into the higher worlds.

But the name itself has even more meaning behind it. I would like to recommend a spiritual exercise which will be very beneficial to you in finding it out for yourself.

As you chant each long, drawn-out HU outwardly, keep asking inwardly, "What is HU?" Repeat the question mentally as many times as is comfortable for you, maybe two or three. In other words, with each outward HU, you are asking within, "What is HU? What is HU? What is HU?"

—Sri Harold Klemp
The Spiritual Exercises of ECK[2]

11
Divine Love in Action

*One of the biggest lessons we can learn in life
is to do everything possible to reach an accord
with the individual we are having trouble with.*

—Harold Klemp, *The Language of Soul*[1]

---

*L*ove brings harmony where hostility once held forth. I've rediscovered this again and again.

When I stood for election to the chairmanship of local government, I was an amateur photographer, and I had a friend who was a professional. We put together a poster that somehow made me look handsomer and more important than I really am. The opposition were not amused.

Poster Palaver

Someone began to tear down my posters every time I put them up. They apparently did not want that handsome, important-looking personality to fool the voters.

The problem was worst on the major road that led to my residence. But try as we might, we could not catch the culprit.

225

One morning, though, as my sister was walking to our house, she caught the fellow red-handed. He was going systematically from one billboard to another, tearing and defacing the posters that my team and I had put up for the umpteenth time. My sister challenged him and then rushed to my house to inform me.

As my assistants and I went up the road to check out the culprit, I sang HU inwardly, asking the Mahanta for guidance so that we could handle this matter with the grace of Divine Spirit.

Tension

A group of motor mechanics had their workshop not more than a hundred meters from my residence. There were about ten of them. The poster destroyer was among them.

As we approached the group, it was obvious that tension had mounted in the place.

"Show me the fellow who has been destroying my posters," I asked my sister when we stood before the group. They now stood silent, muscles tensed, watching and waiting, unsure whether there was going to be physical action here.

She pointed out a stern and battle-scarred, muscular youth, the type who often exhibit plenty of brawn and little else. The fellow in question stood looking belligerent, alternately closing and opening his fists. If a fight was in the offing, he needed to keep his knuckles supple.

"So you're the fellow who has been destroying my posters," I said, looking him in the eye. With bloodshot eyes, he returned my look and said nothing. He was waiting for me to unleash my group on him. Then he would be in his natural element. Everybody had stopped work and was waiting for the free-for-all to commence.

"Whose son are you?"

He named a minor local chief. "Do you know that my wife is from your place?" I asked. She was, in fact.

Friendly Banter

My approach was so unexpected that he began to sweat. He had expected a fight, not friendly banter from someone he was about to fight.

"You didn't write the electoral law, and neither did I," I continued. "The law stipulates that two parties must contend against each other. If I stepped down today, someone else from my party would step in, and he or she would contend against the candidate in your party. So instead of destroying my posters, why don't you bring posters of your party's candidate and paste them side by side with mine?"

This man looked crestfallen, and his feet now drew aimless patterns in the dust. His muscles relaxed, having proven useless in this unaccustomed kind of battle. His fellow mechanics, seeing his discomfiture, began to chuckle, embarrassing him even further.

I thanked him and his mates for giving me audience. Then I advised him to put up posters—any posters— not tear them down.

There was a roar of laughter from the mechanics as we began our walk back to my residence. But the laughter was directed not at us, but at their colleague, who was looking really shamefaced now.

Turned Around

One hour later, there was a knock on our front door. When I opened the door, I saw the poster destroyer standing there.

What now? I wondered.

"You have more of those posters? I'd like to go put them back up!"

He was obviously a man of few words.

It was now my turn to be surprised.

Later, when I got out into town, I discovered that the young man's capacity for putting up posters had by far surpassed his destructive abilities. He had completely turned around. I learned that he even put up my posters in his father's compound, where he lived.

Somebody warned him that his party could sanction him for anti-party activities for putting up posters of the opposing candidate in his house.

"Let them!" he had barked.

White Man's Picture

When I became local government chairman, I took a sixteen-by-twenty-inch (forty-one by fifty-one centimeters) photograph of the Living ECK Master and put it on the wall in my office.

My desk had three official photographs behind it. Every visitor to my office who sat facing me was also facing the pictures of the country's president, our governor, and the paramount chief of our area.

When I brought in the Master's picture, I put it on the opposite wall, where I could look at it every time I was in the office. People sitting opposite me faced the president, governor, and chief, while I faced the Mahanta, the Living ECK Master.

Speculations

When people saw this white man's picture on my wall, there were several speculations about it.

Some said it was the former colonial master who was the first chairman of this place. Others thought I spoke to the picture and received instructions from it. "If the white man tells him to give you a million naira, he won't hesitate!" someone said.

One woman, about to leave my office, went and stood close to the picture. She looked at it and said with vehemence, "Yes, it's *very good* that you put up this picture here!"

That surprised me. But before I could ask her why she said that, she left abruptly.

Who Is This White Man?

A very inquisitive, middle-aged woman came into the office one day when there were many other people present.

"Who is this white man?" she asked loudly.

"A friend," I said.

"What kind of friend?" she insisted.

"A very close one," I responded, smiling.

"It's interesting. I see that the president, governor, and chief are all sitting behind you, while you have this white man up here in the front where he is always in your line of sight," she said. "I think I am going to wait here till everybody leaves the office. Then you can tell me the full story about this white man!"

When the office became empty except for the two of us, she asked me, "Are you a member of Eckankar?" and I answered yes.

"Now I can leave," she said. She'd seen this picture in the private office of another ECKist.

However, the most incredible speculation on the Master's picture in my office came from the labor-union leaders.

Labor Union Strikes

It is not my purpose to indict labor-union leadership in Nigeria. I am only writing about what I had to face.

Out of eighteen local-government councils in the state, mine was one of a handful that did not owe staff salary arrears or allowances.

Through careful planning, within eight months of my tenure, I was able to quash the salary arrears I had inherited from my predecessor. Yet I received more harassment from labor-union officials than most local-government chairmen. Stranger still, hardly any of the strikes planned and executed by the officials of the labor unions followed legal procedures. Having no legal reasons to go on strike, the labor unions turned to more sinister motives.

During one of these illegal strikes, the father of one of the union officials was brought into the negotiation. It was then that I discovered the real reason behind these strikes.

Understanding

The father, after conferring with his son, told me that these union officials felt I "lacked understanding" on the real issues that concerned them. They had spent money on their campaigns to attain their positions, and they expected me to have an "understanding" with them to provide recompense. In short, I was not providing slush funds to buy the cooperation of the top union officials!

"You think paying salaries and hiring contractors is all you are supposed to do here," they complained, "but we spent good money getting into our positions!"

I could now see how it had been possible for my predecessor to withhold the teachers' salaries for three months without the union calling the teachers out on strike even once. He must have been looking after the "priests" of the labor unions very well. That way, he could ignore the "laity" with impunity. This was the culture the union officials expected me to continue during my term of office.

The power of calling workers on strike lay solely with the officials, not the union members.

I have always hated intimidation. I did my job as well as I could, and if the union officials had wanted personal help from me, they ought to have approached me and asked instead of hiding behind illegal strikes to extort concessions for themselves.

Always the Winner

Strangely, though, I always came out the winner after each of these strikes. Halfway through, the strikes would lose steam and collapse without the expected dividends for the leaders.

One day, a report from one of the union officials' meetings was leaked to me. They thought they had found the reason why their strikes were not working out: they fingered the white man's picture!

"Why don't our strikes succeed?" someone had asked in that secret labor-union-leaders' meeting.

"I believe it has something to do with that white man's picture," someone had said. "Next time we start a strike, our first action must be to remove the white man's picture from the wall."

On Rampage

By the last quarter of 1993, both state and local governments in Nigeria owed so much in salary arrears that the president released extra funds for the settlement of such arrears.

I was preparing to go to work one morning when someone brought the news: the National Union of Local Government Employees and the Nigerian Union of Teachers were both on rampage at the local-government secretariat, and they had staged a confrontation.

As usual, there had been no notice whatsoever of a trade dispute, and these events took me completely by surprise.

The person who brought the message suggested that if I had somewhere else to go, I should take a powder.

I was quite amused at this suggestion. How could the head of the house take to his heels when his house is on fire? Who has more interest in putting out the fire than the householder?

Arrested

When I drove onto the premises of the local-government secretariat, the union officials and members couldn't believe their eyes. A great shout rose up as they hand-pushed my car, with me inside, through the sea of striking workers and trapped visitors. I would learn later that my deputy, who was also an ECKist, and all political office holders had been "arrested" and were being detained inside my office. I got out of the car after it was parked in the chairman's carport. Then I prepared to go in and join my fellow detainees.

On the way to my office, I wondered, *Would someone among this lot have actually removed the picture of the Mahanta, the Living ECK Master from the wall as the first action of the "battle"?*

Then I stepped through the door.

My office now had standing room only. But I sat down at my desk, lowered my head, and sang the HU silently for about a minute. Then I raised my eyes and looked over the heads of these invading marauders.

Sri Harold was still there on the wall, chin in hand, watching with an inscrutable smile the sea of politicians, police and union officials, and all who were trapped here.

Inwardly, I winked at him. No use doing that outwardly and warning the union officials that they had failed at the very first step of their battle plan.

They forgot to remove your picture from the wall, I told Sri Harold in my thoughts. I imagined him winking back, chuckling, and saying, "Never trust human memory!"

Reason for the Strike

"What is the reason for this strike?" I asked.

"The deputy governor has released a circular on staff welfare concerning the present release of extra funds," the chairman and spokesman of one of the unions said, "and you have not implemented it."

"Is that all?" I asked. He said it was.

"Well, no one has made the circular available to me," I said.

Someone sent a copy of the circular forward.

When I read it, I smiled inwardly, wondering if any of them had read the circular. I was not unaware how personal greed can blind.

"If I agree, in the presence of these labor-union leaders and security officials, to implement this circular right away, on the spot, will you disband this crowd of striking workers?"

The chairman was about to respond, when somebody sitting next to him pinched him. He bent down, and the other person, who had been perusing the circular, whispered in his ear.

Verbal Demands

"We have other demands," the chairman said.

"Did you include them in your written list of demands?"

"They are verbal. We want vehicle refurbishing loans."

"I thought you had just said, in the presence of

everybody here, that the sole reason for this strike was that I had not implemented the deputy governor's circular," I reminded him.

"We also want vehicle loans," he answered, ignoring my challenge.

"Where is the paper you prepared in which you specified a demand for car loans as part of your trade dispute with us?" I asked.

There was no paper. I had expected none.

The union officials had called their workers out on strike without properly perusing the circular. Someone noticed this when I so readily agreed to implement the circular. They were now scurrying for reasons to save the strike so that they could force me into a secret negotiation that would benefit them. But the deputy governor's circular would prove to be a great embarrassment for the union officials.

On-the-Spot Afterthought

The deputy governor's circular had stipulated that the extra allocations sent to the local-government councils should be used to settle all salary arrears and leave bonuses. But any balance left over—after the arrears and bonuses were paid—was to be used for the day-to-day running of the local government.

As I said before, ours was one of the few local-government councils in the state that had no salary arrears or outstanding leave bonuses to settle.

The union leaders knew that if they accepted the circular as the sole reason for this strike, I would call for the list of salary arrears and leave bonuses. None would be found. I would have implemented the circular without doing anything! Naturally, the strike would collapse.

The fellow who belatedly read through the circular

must have alerted the union chairman to these facts. The car-loans demand was an on-the-spot afterthought. The security officials took note of this trampling of labor laws, and the strike began to lose steam.

Collapse

By eight o'clock that evening, the strike action had collapsed like all the previous ones.

As the union officials, police, and observers trooped out, I looked at the picture of the Mahanta and winked and waved my thanks. This time, I did so with my physical eye and hand. After all, with the help of the Mahanta, I had once again crossed the river despite the labor-union crocodiles.

Picture on the Wall

One curious thing was that everybody *speculated* on the reason I placed the Master's picture on the wall. Not one person *asked* me why. Apparently, many people don't want the truth to tarnish the glitter on their speculation!

The Master's picture in my office was not a talisman to help me divine what I should do while in office. Neither was it a charm against union officials or any other threat.

The Master's picture simply reminded me daily of the ideal I was working for in the tough duty of my office.

The Mahanta, the Living ECK Master is the love of God incarnate!

As events pulled and pushed me here and there, my ideal was to center myself in this divine love and stay level-headed (even when others, like the union officials, lost their heads).

I must have succeeded to an extent.

Rumors

We held an introductory talk for Eckankar in a certain area after I had left the chairmanship. After the intro, a young lady who attended asked me whether there was any truth to the rumors that had been going around during my chairmanship. Apparently it had been rumored that the headquarters of Eckankar in the United States had been steadily sending me US dollars to help "their first political office holder" shine and pull members into Eckankar.

This was laughable. Eckankar does not send money even to build churches or temples for Eckankar, much less for political purposes.

"Why did they speculate so?" I was curious to know.

"How were you able to pay your staff salaries fully and on time, when most local-government chairmen could not?" she asked.

Something More Precious

I now understood what the Mahanta had said in some of his writings: ECK Arahatas (teachers) often have to undo wrong information given to members of the public before they can give them the truth. This was one such case.

It is true that I was getting something from the Mahanta, the Living ECK Master through the teachings of Eckankar. But it was something more precious than American dollars. What I had (and what other chairmen didn't have due to lack of awareness) was the direct love and guidance of the Mahanta.

Politics is an arena where the unprotected and unguided can contract karmic debts so heavy that it could take lifetimes to resolve them. But the love of the Mahanta was always there when I listened and looked for it. When love rules, karma recedes!

Wheelchair Gig

Students of Eckankar study discourses—special letters from the Master—one per month. Eckankar now sends all twelve discourses for a whole year when one subscribes. Back when I came on board, just one discourse per month was sent. And it was then the Mahanta gave me a timely warning: Don't run ahead and steal a peek into other discourses before it is time.

My Initial Interest

The main thing that initially attracted me to Eckankar was not love, the heart of the ECK teachings. It was knowledge. The more I read the ECK discourses, the more knowledge I felt I had. The discourses said some things I did not know before. I loved head knowledge. I quite forgot that these discourses were not designed for head knowledge but to slowly, and in an orderly fashion, open the heart to more divine love.

If all twelve discourses had been dispatched to me at once in those days, I would have ended up rushing ahead to read them all right then out of curiosity, instead of just one per month as instructed. I discovered there could be consequences to such gluttony and lack of self-discipline.

Irregular Discourses

The Nigerian postal system made discourse delivery an irregular affair. One time, lesson 1 came in the mail, then for three months or so I received nothing. When the next envelope arrived in the mail, it contained lesson 4. Where were lessons 2 and 3? The answer was blowing in the wind of the postal service!

What do I do? I wondered. Checking with the Eckankar Spiritual Center, I learned that the Master's instructions were: Read what you have.

As I was reading discourse lesson 4, lessons 2 and 3 dropped out of the mailbox at the same time!

What to do?

At that time, the instruction I received from the Eckankar Spiritual Center was: Read two discourses—your current one and one other—each month till you catch up to the normal rhythm.

But there was also a caution, a caution I found it convenient to ignore: If you are on one discourse and also reading a previous discourse to catch up, do not study a third discourse that month.

But who had ears to hear when *knowledge* lay so enticingly at my fingertips? Besides, the discourses had piled up through no fault of mine. So I found that caution easy to ignore.

I was in for a surprise.

Warning Dreams

First, I began having warning dreams of missing footwear. I would step out to go someplace and realize that somehow I had forgotten to put on my footwear. Sometimes I found them close by, other times, not at all.

At first, I did not understand what these dreams meant. Then I came across a passage in *Ask the Master*, Book 1, where Sri Harold Klemp answers a question from someone who'd been having similar dreams.

The Master explains to the questioner that missing footwear means that the dreamer's inner life has outpaced his outer life. He should set new goals in his daily life to bring the balance back.[2]

I didn't quite get that, so I was given another dream to show me just how out of balance I was.

Game of Life

I am playing tennis. My opponent's side of the tennis court is inside a roofed building. That indoor portion of the tennis court is very long, while the outdoor part of the court where I'm playing is very short. Instead of a net, a flimsy lace cloth covers what looks like a doorway (the Spiritual Eye) *that separates the outer and inner courts.*

The fellow from inside has been serving aces with unbelievable regularity. The ball, which looks more like a badminton shuttle than a tennis ball, flashes through the curtain, bounces within the service line, and sails away before I can react. At the end of the first period, the score is two games in my favor and six in favor of my invisible opponent.

At break time, a sympathetic ECK Master walks with me and explains what had just happened.

That tennis game was the play between my inner and outer lives. The longer part of the court, under cover, was my inner life, and the smaller portion outside was my outer life. The inner had grown disproportionately more than the outer one.

Concerning the score of two to six, my excessive study of the ECK discourses and reading of the ECK books to gain knowledge had pushed my inner life three times faster than my outer life as a Second Initiate could handle! My inner and outer worlds were obviously out of balance.

But unbelievably, I still couldn't make the connection. So the Mahanta gave me more info in another dream.

Handicapped State

I find myself, during my school days, walking toward the countryside to meet a helpful uncle. I had received information along the way, and perhaps even saw my uncle in town. Yet, I proceed with my journey to the wilderness to see him.

I am reading a newspaper. The contents of the newspaper so enthrall me that I have no idea where I am heading. As I continued on, I suddenly find myself in a motorized wheelchair. Yet the sweet contents of the newspaper make me oblivious to my handicapped state.

A brown dog appears, headed in the opposite direction. As it passes me, I feel something pulling my shoulder, trying to drag me back. When I turn around, I discover that the dog has bit into the sleeve of my clothing and is trying to get me to return.

I put my hand into the dog's mouth and grab it by its upper snout, lifting it up and swinging it off the ground. From the torso up, I am very powerful. However, my legs cannot carry me, which is the reason I am wheelchair bound.

I get to a compound with three huts in it, and I shout, "Who owns this dog?" There is no answer. Everybody hides from me as if I am a mad person.

Later, in contemplation, I came to understand this dream.

Wrong Direction

I went looking for the Mahanta—my uncle in the dream—in the "spiritual wilderness." But the Mahanta was in "town"—in the society of humanity, not in the wilderness of imbalance.

The Living ECK Master encourages the student to blend into his or her community and to live a balanced life. My extreme study of the ECK discourses was doing exactly the opposite—taking me away from the community. My imbalance left me with a lack of money and plenty of ill health. Unfit to live in my community,

I had begun to hide from it.

"As you grow in spirituality, your whole life must improve," says Harold Klemp in *The Language of Soul.*[3] But my life had grown worse.

The compound with the three huts was the Causal Plane. I had arrived there hoping to get my next ECK initiation. But the community there looked at my imbalance and turned away in embarrassment. If I was unbalanced on the physical plane, I was just as unbalanced and unwelcome in the inner worlds!

The dog, my dream symbol for divine love, had come to pull me back from the brink. Instead, I demonstrated the false power I had acquired in the "upper body" (mental knowledge from reading) by swinging the dog around even as I remained wheelchair-bound.

Did I stop my wild discourse reading after this dream?

As Nigerians say, *for where?* I made no connection whatsoever between my undisciplined discourse reading and the imbalance my dreams were warning me of. With much love, the Mahanta intervened.

Need to Take a Rest

When it was time to renew my Eckankar membership and receive another discourse series, I trusted a fellow to help with the arrangements. He took my donation and also took a powder! I never saw or heard from him again.

I felt forced to take a break for a year and a half. By the end of that time, a semblance of balance and order began to enter into my life. Only then could I resume my study of the ECK discourses.

It had been a necessary rest, and I was now a much wiser person.

Someone who is out of balance on earth cannot very

well serve God—on earth or in the heavens. Some think the poor will inherit heaven just because they are poor, or that the rich will inherit heaven or hell just because they are rich. Actually the balanced are always in high demand—here and in heaven!

When I was reading too many discourses, I was traveling away from, not toward, the kind of balance that gets one to God. And the Mahanta, out of love, saw fit to intervene in order to lead me back from the wilderness.

Like an African proverb says: Softly, softly, catchee monkey. In other words, if one wants to capture the elusive monkey, one must tread slowly, carefully, and patiently to accomplish the mission.

I find this no less relevant when trying to capture the elusive ECKshar state (Self-Realization) in the climb up the spiritual mountain to the pinnacle of God-Realization!

Dog in the Pool

Harold Klemp tells a story in one of the ECK books about a bear that has a thorn in its paw. The bear is looking for help, but everybody around is afraid of the bear. Then someone drives up, sees the problem, finds a pair of pliers in the car, and pulls the thorn. Later, the grateful bear returns and rewards his helper with two baskets of blueberries.[4]

This kind of story sounds incredible till something similar happens to you. Take my story of a dog in the pool, for instance.

Wild Alsatian

Armed robbers had once attacked my immediate neighbor and members of his family. To protect himself, he later purchased an Alsatian. Because he never intended the animal to be a pet, it was always tethered at the doghouse, away from people. The dog naturally grew up big and wild, just as the owner had intended. If the armed robbers returned, they had better be prepared to get past that wild thing.

A high concrete-block wall separated our two properties. When my neighbor let the dog loose at night, that wall and my chain-link fence kept him out of my yard.

No Gate

When I returned from Gboko to Makurdi after a sojourn of about ten years in politics, I was in a very bad state financially.

A good-hearted neighbor had done some landscape work on adjoining neighborhood properties, and he included my front fence in his landscape development project. He tore down my chain-link fence and the rusty iron entrance gate.

I was grateful for this help. However, during removal of the rusted gate, it fell to pieces. Its replacement became my responsibility. But I had absolutely no finances at the time to replace that gate. So now we lived in a compound without a gate.

Security Situation

People in our town who had walled compounds with locked gates were still vulnerable to armed robberies—as my Alsatian-owning next-door neighbor had found out. But I now had a walled compound without a gate to lock up at night. The security situation was not good.

When people visited my place, they often asked me how I could sleep in that house, knowing that there was no gate to keep criminals out of the compound.

"God provides," I would say. But the truth was we couldn't afford a new gate.

When there's no money for security measures, it's easier to let God be the gatekeeper.

So, there was nothing else we could do but trust in God.

I did not know it at the time, but the Mahanta would use this situation to teach us something about divine love and its lack of limitations.

Fallen Tree

Many unwanted trees had grown in the compound in my absence. Some were threatening the property itself. I couldn't afford to employ people to cut them down, so I began to build fires at the foot of some of them to kill them off. One such tree was next to the fence between me and my neighbor with the fierce dog.

This tree had been attacked by worms from inside and was hollow, but I did not know this. If I had, I would not have burned it for so long.

After the fire at the base of the tree had burned awhile, I heard a sharp report and a crash. This was around seven o'clock one morning.

When I rushed to check, I discovered that the tree had fallen and broken the wall between my Alsatian-owning neighbor's yard and mine.

The tree hit a bull's-eye on the spot where my neighbor usually parked the family Mercedes. Fortunately, for some unknown reason, he had not parked their car there this time. Otherwise, the tree would have destroyed it!

If I could not afford an iron gate, I wonder how I would have afforded paying for a Mercedes-Benz.

The fence between our two properties was now broken and needed urgent repairs. But where were the funds?

My neighbor was very understanding. He had his workers cut branches off the tree that had fallen mostly on his side of the fence and then used these branches as much as he could to block the breach in the wall. Then we both waited for the time when I could afford repairs to the fence.

One night, soon after, I woke up suddenly at around two o'clock in the morning. As I lay in bed, wondering what had woken me, I heard the sound of agitated water. It came from the direction of an uncompleted swimming pool—a project I had started way back in better times but had to abandon when I fell on hard times. I took a torch (flashlight) and went to the backyard to investigate.

Unwise Adventure

When I shone the torch into the pool, which was now nothing more than frog-spawning territory, a large head bobbed above the murky waters. Two beady eyes that belonged to the wild Alsatian stared back at me!

Somehow, he had crossed the breach in the fence and had come to investigate life on our side of the divide. Obviously, it had been an unwise adventure. Not familiar with the geography and treachery of the lay of our land, he had suddenly found himself in the dirty pool, a great offense to his noble breeding. Now this "noble savage" looked—and I believe felt—very, very foolish indeed, swimming helplessly in a stagnant pool. Frogs stared at him in wonderment from the opposite side.

The water was not shallow enough for him to stand on hard ground. Nor was it high enough for him to reach out his front paws to the rim of the pool and climb out.

He must have been there treading water for quite some time, since he now looked not only foolish but also very tired. In another ten or fifteen minutes, he would have been too tired to tread water anymore and would likely have drowned.

You're in Trouble, Sir!

"You're in trouble, sir!" I made the observation with as much respect as I could muster. He tipped his normally alert ears back on his mighty head. His eyes crinkled, and he seemed to try on a tired dog smile. Perhaps he was trying to say something on the order of, "Well, any dog can find himself in some smelly old pool, I believe." He was not just any dog, though, as he would prove later.

"Do I have your permission to *put hand* in this matter?" I inquired in Nigerian English.

Once more, the ears folded back and the eyes crinkled. I assumed that he had agreed. I was right.

Holding the torch in my teeth, I knelt down beside the pool, reached over and hooked my hands under his two powerful forelegs that had proved useless in getting him out of the mess he had got himself into. Then I heaved.

If he didn't weigh as much as a young lion, he was pretty close. But the wild gentleman soon had his feet firmly planted on dry land at last.

Thank You

His first action was to shake the dirty water out of his fur. Next he obeyed an impulse to put the greatest distance possible between himself and that mean, old water hole. However, just as he was about to turn the corner that would have broken the line of sight between us, he remembered his manners.

He halted, turned, and looked in my direction for perhaps five seconds. Then he inclined his mighty head as if to say, "Well, thank you—and sorry for forgetting my manners and dashing off like that." This noble creature was not so savage after all.

Then he was gone.

Prettier Option

I went back to bed, gratified to know I would not wake up in the morning and find his dead body floating in my pool.

When I told the dog owner the story next day, he was astonished.

"Well, if I had not been surprised to find his coat wet this morning," he said, "I would have been hard put to believe your story. It's astounding that this dog would allow a total stranger to get near him, much less put paws on him."

But even though this dog might have been wild enough to serve his owner's security needs, he proved to me that he was not foolish. He knew his limits as Soul in a physical body.

The dog had decided that between the Angel of Death and my straggly mustachioed face, I looked like the prettier option. And so he allowed a total stranger— me—to haul him out of a dirty water hole that was about to snuff out his life.

I did not add to the neighbor's incredulity by letting him know his dog had paused for a few seconds to say thank you. His beliefs did not allow for that sort of behavior from an animal, no matter how noble.

But this dog was not finished with me yet.

Dog Patrol

One night, I awoke from my dreams into a Soul Travel experience. The clarity of the experience surpassed the waking state of reality.

A number of dogs stood guard in my gateless compound. As I walked around, wondering what to make of this scene, something grabbed my hand. I turned and saw the intense look of my next-door neighbor's wild dog. He was looking up at me as if to say, "Remember this face? I almost drowned in your dirty pool." By seizing my hand, he had just made a mock arrest. It was partly to get me to notice him and partly to show why he was here: he was on guard duty in my compound!

It was only play-acting, but this fellow apparently didn't know how much strength he had in his jaws. "Hey! Hey! Hey!" I joked, imitating Eddie Murphy, "Go easy now on that hand, eh!"

The reality soon dawned on me. The dog next door was so grateful for being saved from drowning in that dirty pool that he returned on the inner planes, arranging a dog patrol to secure my gateless compound!

Some might sniff at a security operation mounted on inner planes, but they forget that before anything (including a robbery) can occur physically, on the outer, it must first pass through the inner worlds. That dog knew this. Keep the place safe on the inner, and physical security becomes a fait accompli! I suspect this is one method the ECK Masters may use at times to protect others.

My compound stayed without a gate for about a year. We were never robbed or burgled even once.

Divine Love and the Law of Economy

Divine love is the spiritual Law of Economy in operation.

The tree fell and broke the fence, but it missed the neighbor's car—a liability I could have ill afforded. The broken fence brought the dog. If the dog had drowned, it would have been a misfortune he and his owner could have ill afforded.

However, this seeming mistake afforded opportunities for the dog and me to get our spiritual lessons and give service in ways we could both afford and benefit from. He learned humility, and I got the security guard I needed.

It also reconfirmed to me that animals are Soul too!

Sri Harold Klemp has said so, and there is even an Eckankar book by him with that title (*Animals Are Soul Too!*). Now I know it firsthand.

Father's Funeral

My father translated (died) in November 1998. The time leading up to his translation saw a running battle between us. I am afraid I wasn't as graceful about the situation as I should have been. I talked when I should have kept quiet. Talking back at my father created a karmic debt that would subsist even after his death. I would see pepper!

Psychic Time Bomb

During his life, my father was aware that we were both sitting on a ticking psychic time bomb. The Mahanta made me aware of the psychic debts we owed, and my father was also aware of them to an extent. But here the similarities between us ended.

I knew the reason that I reincarnated here, in this lifetime when I would meet the Mahanta, was partly to untie some of the psychic knots I had put in place in certain past lives. With the protection of the Mahanta, I knew nothing would happen to me or my family that shouldn't.

But to my father, psychics were like the mafia: In the end, they'd get you.

Without the Mahanta, I could not have agreed with my father more. To me, the Mahanta made all the difference. But my father reckoned that we had no psychic strength or protection in this life, since we ourselves were not even psychic.

People within the kindred attributed my success in education, business, and politics to the effects of the psychic altars in our family lineage.

In the West, people struggle over material inheritance. In our society, the struggle over psychic artifacts can be just as intense. But these battles are beyond the jurisdiction of the judicial system.

There was jealousy within the sub-kindred, and my father, who lived in the village, knew it. Some of my father's sub-kindred "brothers" felt that they were less successful simply because I was so successful!

The psychic attacks on me started even before my present body was born. My mother was in labor for five days, and there was no hospital in the area at the time. When I was born alive, it was considered a birth that had beaten incredible odds.

A Tough Period

As the jealousy grew around us, my father became very afraid. His suggestion was flight—a permanent departure from the area.

I had a different opinion. And that is where the friction between us arose.

"When I die and leave you with these people, I have my doubts if you could handle them," he said a month before he translated. He added angrily that after his death, our kinsmen would not only send me to an early grave, they would also ruin the rest of his family—all because of my hardheadedness in refusing to go into exile as he advised.

It was a tough period for both of us.

I should have kept quiet. Unfortunately, I didn't. I angered my father more by throwing in some well-chosen words that he could not argue his way around. At one point, he even put a curse on my efforts in politics!

Useless Son

After his death, my father returned to my sister's place in the Astral body and sat there, refusing to move on to where he should go. When I visited him in the dream state and greeted him, he ignored me. He pointed to a large bird sitting in the mango tree under which he sat and asked me if I heard what the bird said. When I said I did not, he told me the bird said I was a useless son.

My father resisted having his body interred in the family cemetery where my mother, uncle, aunt, and others before him had been interred. Hence, the burial arrangements kept falling apart. After some time, people began to speculate that I had buried my father's body elsewhere and was only biding my time, preparing to move the rest of the family away—as my father had wanted.

Later, when the burial date was firmly fixed, the new kindred spokesman (who had taken that position over from my father) confessed something to me. He had decided that if I buried my father elsewhere, they would have demanded that I exhume all the other bodies from their land and bury them wherever I had taken my father's body!

The Mahanta Intervened

My father's continued resistance, on the inner, to the burial of his body in the family cemetery canceled out every effort I made to raise funds for a ceremony befitting his role as kindred spokesman. Each and every wealthy friend who tried to come to my aid suddenly developed some financial problem that made him or her withdraw.

It was at this time that the Mahanta intervened.

Nightly, he took me into the other worlds to go meet

my father so we could come to an amicable solution to this impasse. By then, I had developed more grace and didn't talk back at him even when he made provocative comments.

One night the Mahanta advised me to take along a casket in the trunk of my car.

Ready to Move

During our jovial moods, I used to call my father by his nickname, Old Rickety Bicycle.

In his youth, he was a dashing young man who was also quick to come to blows with those who trifled with him. So his age-mates named him Old Rickety Bicycle. Every time he was called by that name, he would respond, "Zouloo!" It meant you had better ride him very carefully if you did not wish to end up in the dirt!

Apparently I had forgotten to ride him carefully. I was already in the dirt, and I would have remained there, had the Mahanta not intervened.

When I arrived that night with the casket, I called out, "Old Rickety Bicycle." My father got up silently and, with a half smile, began putting on his large gown. He was finally ready to move on in the inner worlds where he now belonged.

After that dream, the wherewithal to bury him began to trickle in. When I finally buried his body, my father had been dead for one hundred and ten days!

In the end, even the dour mortuary attendant took pity on me. He cut my mortuary fees by almost half. It was the second-largest gift for the burial!

Try this spiritual exercise today!

Count Your Blessings

This technique involves attitude, and it is one that must be lived. In a word, it's called *gratitude*.

Throughout the day, contemplate on all the blessings in your life. The power of gratitude opens the heart to allow love to enter. But once the love comes in and we receive the gifts of Divine Spirit and of life, the way to keep the gifts flowing is to be grateful.

—Sri Harold Klemp
The Spiritual Exercises of ECK[5]

12
Perfect Poem

The law which all seek to know is the great principle of life. Its simplicity is amazing for it is summed up in the statement: Soul exists because God loves It. In other words, all life exists because God so wills it. This is the very foundation of life, the whole of the philosophy of Eckankar. There is nothing more and nothing less. All life is built upon this basic principle of God. If Soul did not exist, there would be no life anywhere on earth or on any of the planets, nor on the various and many planes throughout the universe of God.

If the chela could only grasp this very simple principle of life, he would have the entire philosophy of Eckankar in his hand.

—*The Shariyat-Ki-Sugmad*, Books One & Two[1]

More than two decades back, I read a story in *Reader's Digest* about a man who bought a guitar.

Day in, day out, he pressed his fingers to a single spot on the neck of the instrument and kept strumming away, bliss washing over his face.

His wife soon grew tired of this changeless music.

"Whenever I see others play that instrument," the wife pointed out, "I see them move their hand up and down the neck."

"The reason they are moving their hand up and down the neck," he answered promptly, "is because they are looking for the right spot. I have found it!"

Perfect Poem

At the time I read that story, I thought it was just dry humor. But then, one morning just as I was about to wake up, I had the following inner experience.

Six Words

Someone held what at first looked like the printed page of a newspaper in front of me. Circled with a black or dark-blue felt pen were six words. When I read the circled words, I was astounded.

The author of these words had done what is virtually impossible: In just six words, he had summed up eternity!

I wish I could express the fullness of this experience in human language. But alas, it is not possible.

Tears of joy welled up in my eyes as I drank in the beauty of those six words.

Nothing to Add, Nothing to Subtract

There was nothing to add and nothing to subtract. All eternity rested in those six words!

They comprised a perfect poem.

To live in the bliss of those words was to halt all seeking.

To live in them banished outside and inside.

Fear ceased; up or down disappeared; and bad or

good, light and shadow were no more.

All tomorrows, today, and yesterdays compressed into a singularity of pure being.

Was this the legendary end of the rainbow?

I knew that I had come to *Finality*, the halting of all seeking, and I wanted to remain *here* forever—a fitting end to a long journey through the heavens.

All my friends must hear these incredible words, I promised myself. It was one of those moments in the inner worlds when I wished I had some kind of camera or Xerox machine that could capture the experience so I could bring it to the outer world.

Then a kind hand rested on my shoulder and began to lead me away from that "newspaper." I wanted to stay, to protest, but it was no use. So I greedily tried to memorize the six words. Then I awakened fully in my physical body.

Lost and Found

I couldn't believe it: I was unable to recall even the first letter of the first word.

What language had it been written in?

How was it possible to have completely forgotten such beauty in the twinkling of an eye?

I walked around in sadness for a week, nursing my loss.

Then about a week after that inner experience, I picked up the bible of Eckankar, *The Shariyat-Ki-Sugmad*, Book One. I settled down to read and opened it at random to page 142.

As I read, I came to a short passage in the middle of the page and halted. Why did these words suddenly light up for me: "Soul exists because God loves It."

It was the words that followed which finally drove the point home:

> In other words, all life exists because God so wills it. This is the very foundation of life, the whole of the philosophy of Eckankar. There is nothing more and nothing less. All life is built upon this basic principle of God.[2]

The penny finally dropped.

Why, these were the six lost-but-now-found words circled in that "newspaper" article!

But why was reading these six words so totally and intensely blissful in that inner experience?

The Master Moved to Tears

An article about the 2003 ECK Worldwide Seminar in the December 2003 *Mystic World* (a quarterly publication for members of Eckankar) included the report of a woman who saw the Master moved to tears when he listened to the HU sung by the audience just as he walked onstage. She had asked the Inner Master what that experience was like.

At first, one might wonder why she would even ask that question. After all, she was also listening to the HU sung by the audience.

My understanding is that the woman, at the time she put the question to the Inner Master, was listening to the HU song with just her outer ears while the Master did so with his inner ears as well. To help her hear what had moved him to tears, the Master opened her inner ears.

Then, the article says, "Suddenly the sound of HU sung by a heavenly choir filled her. It stayed with her as Sri Harold spoke."[3]

I Had Become What I Read!

And so, once more, why was reading those six words in the inner experience so totally and intensely blissful?

I realized that in there, the Mahanta had not only opened my faculties to see, hear, and comprehend; it had been a total-immersion experience for me. For a brief moment, I had *become* what I read!

Sing HU to Become God's Love

"Soul exists because God loves It."

The Mahanta showed me that the truth of those six words from the Shariyat-Ki-Sugmad can be found in the love song to God:

HU.

The Sound behind all Sounds.

Try singing HU yourself. Perhaps the Master will open your inner ears or inner sight so you can see and hear what brought tears of joy to his eyes.

You might also shed your own tears of joy—in your own way!

Try this spiritual exercise always!

Just open your heart to divine love, sing HU, and remember:

Love comes to those who give love.[4]

Next Steps in Spiritual Exploration

- **Try a spiritual exercise** on a daily basis. Example: With eyes open or closed, take a few deep breaths to relax. Then begin to sing HU (pronounced like the word *hue*) in a long, drawn-out sound, HU-U-U-U. Take another breath, and sing HU again. Continue for up to twenty minutes. Sing HU with a feeling of love, and it will gradually open your heart to God.

- **Browse our Web site: www.Eckankar.org.** Watch videos, get free books, answers to FAQs, and more info.

- **Attend an Eckankar event** in your area. Visit "Eckankar around the World" on our Web site.

- **Read additional books** about the ECK teachings.

- **Explore an advanced spiritual study class** (or study privately) with the Eckankar discourses that come with membership.

Books

If you would like to read additional books by Harold Klemp about the ECK teachings, you may find these of special interest. They are available at bookstores, online booksellers, or directly from Eckankar.

The Call of Soul

Harold Klemp takes you on an amazing journey into a world you may have only dared to dream of—the infinite world of God's love for you. More, he shows, through spiritual exercises, dream techniques, and Soul Travel explorations, how this love translates into every event, relationship, and moment of your life. Includes a CD with dream and Soul Travel techniques.

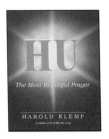

HU, the Most Beautiful Prayer

The simple spiritual exercises in this book will open your heart to see God's loving presence in your life. Includes a CD with the sound of thousands of people singing this powerful, majestic love song to God. Read, listen, or sing along. It lifts you spiritually, no matter your age, background, or religion.

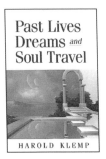

Past Lives, Dreams, and Soul Travel

These stories and exercises help you find your true purpose, discover greater love than you've ever known, and learn that spiritual freedom is within reach.

The Spiritual Exercises of ECK

This book is a staircase with 131 steps leading to the doorway to spiritual freedom, self-mastery, wisdom, and love. A comprehensive volume of spiritual exercises for every need.

How to Survive Spiritually in Our Times, Mahanta Transcripts, Book 16

Discover how to reinvent yourself spiritually—to thrive in a changing world. Stories, tools, techniques, and spiritual insights to apply in your life now.

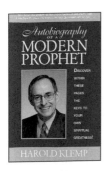

Autobiography of a Modern Prophet

This riveting story of Harold Klemp's climb up the Mountain of God will help you discover the keys to your own spiritual greatness.

Those Wonderful ECK Masters

Would you like to have *personal* experience with spiritual masters that people all over the world—since the beginning of time—have looked to for guidance, protection, and divine love? This book includes real-life stories and spiritual exercises to meet eleven ECK Masters.

The Spiritual Laws of Life

Learn how to keep in tune with your true spiritual nature. Spiritual laws reveal the behind-the-scenes forces at work in your daily life.

Advanced Spiritual Study

Advanced spiritual study is available through yearly membership in Eckankar. This annual cycle of study and practice focuses on the ECK discourses, which may be studied privately or in a class. Each year the spiritual student decides whether to continue with his or her studies in Eckankar.

Discourses

As you study the teachings of ECK, you will find a series of changes in your heart and mind that can make you a better, stronger, and more happy person. Each month of the year, you'll study a new discourse and practice a new technique to enhance your spiritual journey.

The twelve lessons in *The Easy Way Discourses* by Harold Klemp include these titles and more: "In Soul You Are Free," "Dream On, Sweet Dreamer," "Reincarnation—Why You Came to Earth Again," "The Master Principle," and "The God Worlds—Where No One Has Gone Before?"

How to Get Started

To request information about ECK books or to sign up for ECK membership and get your advanced spiritual study discourses along with other membership benefits (renewable annually), you may:

- Visit www.ECKBooks.org
- Join online at "Membership" at www.Eckankar.org (click on "Online Membership Application"), or
- Call Eckankar (952) 380-2222 to apply, or
- Write to:
  ECKANKAR, Att: Information, BK 93
  PO Box 2000
  Chanhassen, MN 55317-2000 USA

Glossary

Words set in SMALL CAPS are defined elsewhere in this glossary.

Arahata. *ah-rah-HAH-tah* An experienced and qualified teacher of ECKANKAR classes.

Blue Light. How the MAHANTA often appears in the inner worlds to the CHELA or seeker.

chela. *CHEE-lah* A spiritual student. Often refers to a member of ECKANKAR.

ECK. *EHK* The Life Force, the Holy Spirit, or Audible Life Current which sustains all life.

Eckankar. *EHK-ahn-kahr* Religion of the Light and Sound of God. Also known as the Ancient Science of SOUL TRAVEL. A truly spiritual religion for the individual in modern times. The teachings provide a framework for anyone to explore their own spiritual experiences. Established by PAUL TWITCHELL, the modern-day founder, in 1965. The word means Co-worker with God.

ECK Master(s). Spiritual Masters who can assist and protect people in their spiritual studies and travels. The ECK Masters are from a long line of God-Realized SOULS who know the responsibility that goes with spiritual freedom.

Fubbi Quantz. *FOO-bee KWAHNTS* The guardian of the SHARIYAT-KI-SUGMAD at the Katsupari Monastery in northern Tibet. He was the MAHANTA, the LIVING ECK MASTER during the time of Buddha, about 500 BC.

God-Realization. The state of God Consciousness. Complete and conscious awareness of God.

Gopal Das. *GOH-pahl DAHS* The guardian of the SHARIYAT-KI-SUGMAD at the Temple of Asklepsis on the Astral PLANE. He was the MAHANTA, the LIVING ECK MASTER in Egypt, about 3000 BC.

HU. *HYOO*   The most ancient, secret name for God. The singing of the word *HU* is considered a love song to God. It can be sung aloud or silently to oneself.

initiation.   Earned by a member of ECKANKAR through spiritual unfoldment and service to God. The initiation is a private ceremony in which the individual is linked to the Sound and Light of God.

Kal Niranjan. *KAL nee-RAHN-jahn*   The Kal; the negative power, also known as Satan or the devil.

Karma, Law of.   The Law of Cause and Effect, action and reaction, justice, retribution, and reward, which applies to the lower or psychic worlds: the Physical, Astral, Causal, Mental, and Etheric PLANES.

Klemp, Harold.   The present MAHANTA, the LIVING ECK MASTER. SRI Harold Klemp became the Mahanta, the Living ECK Master in 1981. His spiritual name is WAH Z.

Living ECK Master.   The title of the spiritual leader of ECKANKAR. His duty is to lead SOUL back to God. The Living ECK Master can assist spiritual students physically as the Outer Master, in the dream state as the Dream Master, and in the spiritual worlds as the Inner Master. SRI HAROLD KLEMP became the MAHANTA, the Living ECK Master in 1981.

Mahanta. *mah-HAHN-tah*   A title to describe the highest state of God Consciousness on earth, often embodied in the LIVING ECK MASTER. He is the Living Word. An expression of the Spirit of God that is always with you. Sometimes seen as a BLUE LIGHT or Blue Star or in the form of the Mahanta, the Living ECK Master.

planes.   The levels of existence, such as the Physical, Astral, Causal, Mental, Etheric, and SOUL Planes.

Rebazar Tarzs. *REE-bah-zahr TAHRZ*   A Tibetan ECK MASTER known as the Torchbearer of ECKANKAR in the lower worlds.

Satsang. *SAHT-sahng*   A class in which students of ECK study a monthly lesson from ECKANKAR.

Self-Realization.   SOUL recognition.   The entering of SOUL into the Soul PLANE and there beholding Itself as pure Spirit. A state of seeing, knowing, and being.

Shariyat-Ki-Sugmad. *SHAH-ree-aht-kee-SOOG-mahd*   The sacred scriptures of ECKANKAR. The scriptures are comprised of about twelve volumes in the spiritual worlds. The first two were transcribed from the inner PLANES by PAUL TWITCHELL, modern-day founder of ECKANKAR.

Soul.   The True Self. The inner, most sacred part of each person. Soul exists before birth and lives on after the death of the physical body. As a spark of God, Soul can see, know, and perceive all things. It is the creative center of Its own world.

Soul Travel.   The expansion of consciousness. The ability of SOUL to transcend the physical body and travel into the spiritual worlds of God. Soul Travel is taught only by the LIVING ECK MASTER. It helps people unfold spiritually and can provide proof of the existence of God and life after death.

Sound and Light of ECK.   The Holy Spirit. The two aspects through which God appears in the lower worlds. People can experience them by looking and listening within themselves and through SOUL TRAVEL.

Spiritual Exercises of ECK.   The daily practice of certain techniques to get us in touch with the Light and Sound of God.

Sri. *SREE*   A title of spiritual respect, similar to reverend or pastor, used for those who have attained the Kingdom of God. In ECKANKAR, it is reserved for the MAHANTA, the LIVING ECK MASTER.

Sugmad. *SOOG-mahd*   A sacred name for God. Sugmad is neither masculine nor feminine; It is the source of all life.

Temples of Golden Wisdom.   These Golden Wisdom Temples are spiritual temples which exist on the various PLANES—from the Physical to the Anami Lok; CHELAS of ECKANKAR are taken to the temples in the SOUL body to be educated in the divine knowledge; the different sections of the SHARIYAT-KI-SUGMAD, the sacred teachings of ECK, are kept at these temples.

Twitchell, Paul.   An American ECK MASTER who brought the modern teachings of ECKANKAR to the world through his writings and lectures. His spiritual name is Peddar Zaskq.

vairag. *vie-RAHG*   Detachment.

Wah Z. *WAH zee*   The spiritual name of SRI HAROLD KLEMP. It means the secret doctrine. It is his name in the spiritual worlds.

Yaubl Sacabi. *YEEOW-buhl sah-KAH-bee* Guardian of the SHARIYAT-KI-SUGMAD in the spiritual city of Agam Des. He was the MAHANTA, the LIVING ECK MASTER in ancient Greece.

For more explanations of ECKANKAR terms, see *A Cosmic Sea of Words: The ECKANKAR Lexicon* by Harold Klemp.

Notes

Introduction

1. *The Shariyat-Ki-Sugmad,* Books One & Two (Minneapolis: ECKANKAR, 1970, 1987; 1971, 1988), 112.

Part One: Encounter with the Chief Agent of God
Chapter 1. Wake-Up Calls

1. Harold Klemp, *How to Survive Spiritually in Our Times,* Mahanta Transcripts, Book 16 (Minneapolis: ECKANKAR, 2001), 42.
2. *The Shariyat-Ki-Sugmad,* Books One & Two, 75–76.
3. Harold Klemp, *The Spiritual Exercises of ECK,* 3rd ed. (Minneapolis: ECKANKAR, 1993, 1997), 15.

Chapter 2. Face-to-Face

1. *The Shariyat-Ki-Sugmad,* Books One & Two, 96.
2. Ibid., 311.
3. "Ten Thousand Hear the Living Word in Africa" in *The Mystic World* (Minneapolis: ECKANKAR, Winter 1991).
4. Klemp, *The Spiritual Exercises of ECK,* 267.

Part Two: Travels from Earth into the Heavens
Chapter 3. Spiritual Matriculation

1. *The Shariyat-Ki-Sugmad,* Books One & Two, 100.
2. Harold Klemp, *The Living Word,* Book 1 (Minneapolis: ECKANKAR, 1989), 169–70.
3. Klemp, *The Spiritual Exercises of ECK,* 237.

Chapter 4. Pink Road to Heaven

1. *The Shariyat-Ki-Sugmad,* Books One & Two, 330.
2. "What I Did for Love" in *Earth to God: Come In Please . . .* (Minneapolis: ECKANKAR, 1991), 183–86.
3. Klemp, *The Spiritual Exercises of ECK,* 39.

Chapter 5. Twisting the Tail of Destiny

1. *The Shariyat-Ki-Sugmad*, Books One & Two, 34.
2. Harold Klemp, *The Art of Spiritual Dreaming* (Minneapolis: ECKANKAR, 1999), 243.
3. Klemp, *The Spiritual Exercises of ECK*, 39–40.

Chapter 6. Mind over Matter

1. *The Shariyat-Ki-Sugmad*, Books One & Two, 467–68.
2. Ibid., 468.
3. Harold Klemp, *The Book of ECK Parables*, Volume 2 (Minneapolis: ECKANKAR, 1988), 33–34.
4. Harold Klemp, *A Cosmic Sea of Words: The ECKANKAR Lexicon*, 2nd ed (Minneapolis: ECKANKAR, 1998, 2009), 225.
5. Phil Morimitsu, *In the Company of ECK Masters*, (Minneapolis: Phil Morimitsu, 1987), 163–68.
6. *The Shariyat-Ki-Sugmad*, Books One & Two, 321.
7. Paul Twitchell, *The ECK-Vidya, Ancient Science of Prophecy* (Minneapolis: ECKANKAR, 1972), 27–28.
8. Ibid., 32.
9. Ibid., 159.
10. Harold Klemp, *Wisdom of the Heart*, Book 2 (Minneapolis: ECKANKAR, 1999), 52.
11. Harold Klemp, *The Eternal Dreamer*, Mahanta Transcripts, Book 7 (Minneapolis: ECKANKAR, 1992), 30–31.
12. Klemp, *The Spiritual Exercises of ECK*, 40.

Chapter 7. Subconscious Spam

1. Klemp, *The Art of Spiritual Dreaming*, 87.
2. Harold Klemp, *Wisdom of the Heart*, Book 1 (Minneapolis: ECKANKAR, 1992), 30.
3. Harold Klemp, *What Is Spiritual Freedom?* Mahanta Transcripts, Book 11 (Minneapolis: ECKANKAR, 1995), 35–36.
4. *The Shariyat-Ki-Sugmad*, Books One & Two, 331.

Part Three : The Supremacy of Love and Service

Chapter 8. Love and Service

1. Harold Klemp, *The Secret of Love*, Mahanta Transcripts, Book 14 (Minneapolis: ECKANKAR, 1996), 26.
2. Klemp, *The Spiritual Exercises of ECK*, 199.

Chapter 9. Wisdom

1. *The Shariyat-Ki-Sugmad*, Books One & Two, 407–8.
2. Klemp, *The Spiritual Exercises of ECK*, 121.

Chapter 10. The Gift of HU

1. Paul Twitchell, *The Flute of God* (Minneapolis: ECKANKAR, 1969), 84.
2. Klemp, *The Spiritual Exercises of ECK*, 103.

Chapter 11. Divine Love in Action

1. Harold Klemp, *The Language of Soul* (Minneapolis: ECKANKAR, 2003), 72.
2. Harold Klemp, *Ask the Master*, Book 1 (Minneapolis: ECKANKAR, 1993), 16.
3. Klemp, *The Language of Soul*, 8.
4. Harold Klemp, *The Book of ECK Parables*, Volume 2 (Minneapolis: ECKANKAR, 1988), 165–66
5. Klemp, *The Spiritual Exercises of ECK*, 13.

Chapter 12. Perfect Poem

1. *The Shariyat-Ki-Sugmad*, Books One & Two, 142.
2. Ibid., 142.
3. *The Mystic World* (Minneapolis: ECKANKAR, December 2003).
4. *The Shariyat-Ki-Sugmad*, Books One & Two, 124.